How to Settle an Estate in Scotland – A Practical Guide

Second Edition

Stephanie is a private client solicitor and notary public who has specialised exclusively with estate administration, Wills, incapacity law, trusts, succession & Inheritance Tax planning for high net worth and ultra high net worth individuals across the UK since 2004.

Stephanie started her career in private practice with Edinburgh firm Henderson Boyd Jackon WS (now Addleshaw Goddard) before moving back to Glasgow with Brechin Tindal Oatts. From there, she moved in house to global accountancy firm, Mazars in 2007 where she assisted with the development of their in-house private client offering. From there, she became Managing Director with EBS Trustees Limited in 2016, one of Scotland's oldest Will writing & private trust companies, before becoming a freelance Consultant Solicitor in 2020 and a Director with Curle Stewart Limited heading up their Private Client Team in 2024.

Stephanie was born and raised in Glasgow, Scotland. Stephanie studied Business Law and graduated with a BA Hons from the University of Strathclyde before returning to complete her LLB and Post Graduate Diploma in Legal Practice.

As well as being a current member of the Law Society of Scotland, Stephanie is also a Notary Public and a full member of STEP (The Society of Trusts and Estates Practitioners), an internationally recognised association for private client professionals. Stephanie has also completed STEP diplomas in both Scottish and English Wills, Trusts and Estates as well as their Advanced Certificate in Will Writing which she obtained with distinction.

Stephanie's client base crosses all ages and backgrounds – the young, the old, entrepreneurs, owner managers and intergenerational wealth. They are all at different stages in their lives and all have different goals. The one thing they have in common is that they want to know that their hard earned wealth is looked after and passed to future generations in a secure and tax efficient manner. Stephanie enjoys putting in place succession plans for her clients, and enjoys creating flexible plans which can move and grow as the client's family circumstances change. Stephanie also advises on exit strategies for businesses to maximise wealth extraction for the owner and their families. Likewise, Stephanie acts as Executor for many of her long-term clients.

Stephanie has administered over 200 active family trusts during her career. Stephanie currently manages more than 50 trusts, as well as acting as a trustee for a number of her clients.

In addition to her private client base, Stephanie also receives referrals from other solicitors and law firms to advise on and deal with complex estate administration matters.

Stephanie regularly speaks to business and community groups on succession planning, incapacity law and trusts. A well kent face in the West of Scotland business community, Stephanie is also a regular contributor to Quality FM's "Legal Matters" program.

Stephanie is also the author of "A Practical Guide to Administering Estates and Obtaining Probate in England & Wales" which is also available from Law Brief Publishing.

Follow Stephanie on LinkedIn at:
https://www.linkedin.com/in/stephaniechristiecarmichael/

How to Settle an Estate in Scotland – A Practical Guide

Second Edition

Stephanie Christie-Carmichael

BA (Hons), LLB (Scots), Dip LP, NP, TEP

Law Brief Publishing

Published 2025 by Law Brief Publishing, an imprint of Law Brief Publishing Ltd
30 The Parks
Minehead
Somerset
TA24 8BT

www.lawbriefpublishing.com

Paperback: 978-1-916698-79-6

For Luke and Joshua EC

There will always be people looking to rain on your parade.

Use an umbrella and jump in the puddles.

PREFACE

If you are looking for a book on how the history of the law on estate administration has evolved or the intricacies of section so and so of an Act of Parliament, please turn to the back of the book, look at the further reading section and pick a book from there. This is not the book for you. If you are looking for a book that deals with the practical nuts and bolts of administering an estate in Scotland, I invite you to please read on!

This book is designed to give the general practitioner, solicitors who don't normally deal with estates and trainee solicitors a guide to dealing with the practical and effective administration of an estate in Scotland. It won't (can't) cover everything but it should give you enough information to at least be comfortable managing an estate on behalf of a client and knowing where to look for further information.

The law is described was believed to be accurate and up to date at 28th February 2025.

Stephanie Christie-Carmichael
February 2025

ACKNOWLEDGEMENTS

It was a bit of a heady experience when I first sat down to write the first edition of this book. Even more so, when I was advised by the fantastic people at Law Brief Publishing that my book had sold enough copies to warrant a second edition! Thanks are very much due to Tim and Garry at Law Brief Publishing for agreeing to publish the first edition of this book in the first place and starting me on my writing journey and second of all, for all of their guidance and encouragement in bringing this second edition to life. Thanks are also due to Cameron McKnight, trainee solicitor at Curle Stewart Limited for bringing (dragging!) this technophobe into the 21st Century! Last but by no means least, thank you to the folks out there who bought my first book. Without you, this second edition would not have happened.

CONTENTS

CHAPTER ONE

PRELIMINARY MATTERS

It is a sad fact of life that to deal with the administration of an estate, there has to be a death. If my 20 years or so experience in law has taught me anything, grief will affect people in a variety of ways. Some people become uber efficient and want the estate dealt with immediately so they can obtain closure on the experience. Other people will put off dealing with the administration of an estate until circumstances force them to accept the person has died and deal with the assets (or the debts as the case may be). Occasionally you find the estate administration had been put off that long, the person entitled to deal with the estate has also died, and you have not one but two (and in some cases more!) estates to deal with to get the assets to the right place. Some people will cry their way through the experience while others may appear flippant, angry or just downright rude. As an estate administrator, you will have to deal with every emotion a person has, and compared to any other area of law, you need to have compassion for what people are going through, particularly when their behaviour may not be that of a normal client. If you are not a "people person", this is not going to be the area of law for you.

<u>Incidental Financial Services Business</u>

If you are going to deal in estates, in addition to the usual master policy insurance, you should also obtain a license to undertake incidental financial services business from the Law Society of Scotland. This will be particularly important if you are procuring Bonds of Caution (pronounced kay-shun) for intestate estates for your clients. You may be dealing with selling and transferring investments and making claims on bonds, life insurance etc. You may need to involve financial advisers to provide advice to your Executors, particularly if you are looking at potentially timing the liquidation of assets to take advantage of Executor tax allowances.

You will require to set out in separate correspondence to your clients, certain regulatory information when purchasing Bonds of Caution, Insurance or buying or selling investments. Template client information can be found at Rules C.2.6-8 of the Law Society of Scotland rules.

Further information on incidental financial services business can be found at https://www.lawscot.org.uk/members/rules-and-guidance/rules-and-guidance/section-c/rule-c2/guidance/c2-incidental-financial-business-generally/

Who is your client?

When dealing with a death, more often than not, your client is the Executor. For the avoidance of doubt, this book has been designed to deal with estates where your Client is the Executor, although you may find it helpful if your client is a beneficiary who is unhappy with progress made by an Executor.

For testate estates (where there is a Will), this will be:

1. the person(s)/organisation(s) named as Executor in the Will;

2. anyone else assumed into the role by the named Executors;

3. where all Executors have died, resigned or declined to act as Executor, it will usually be the residuary beneficiaries who will end up in that role[1].

For intestate estates (where there is no Will), this will be the person or persons entitled to be appointed as Executor Dative. The order of who

[1] S3 Executors (Scotland) Act 1903; See Currie on Confirmation, 9th Edition, Eilidh Scobbie for further information.

can be appointed as Executor Dative follows the laws of intestate succession[2] as follows:

1. Where the prior rights of a spouse/civil partner[3] exhaust the whole estate or where the deceased was not survived by children or remoter descendents, the person so entitled to be discerned will be the spouse/civil partner.

2. Where the prior rights of a spouse/civil partner do not exhaust the whole estate and there are children of the deceased, the person so entitled to be discerned will be the spouse/civil partner or one or more children or a mixture of both;

3. If there is no spouse/civil partner, then the order of who can be appointed will follow the laws of succession on intestacy namely the children of the deceased, remoter issue of the deceased, siblings and/or parents of the deceased and their issue, aunts and uncles, cousins and will continue to go back up the family tree until eventually someone is found who can act as Executor.

4. If there is no family member who can be traced, the estate will pass to the Crown as Ultimus Haeres. In this situation, you should contact the National Ultimus Haeres Unit[4] for guidance before proceeding any further.

In some cases, the person who comes to you to advise you of the death may expect to be Executor. With intestate estates, it is always best to have a genealogist check the family tree that has been provided to ensure you are instructed by the person with title to act. A list (which is by no means exclusive) of genealogists has been provided at the back of this book. All

---

2 S2 Succession (Scotland) Act 1964 as amended

3 S8-9A Succession (Scotland) Act 1964 as amended.

4 See the useful addresses section at the back of this book

of them offer family tree checking services[5]. If you are going to put together a family tree for checking, try and collect as much information as you can regarding names, dates of birth, adoption, marriage, death and divorce and last known areas of residence.

Beneficiaries will often believe they are the client. They are not unless they are also the Executor. Where a beneficiary is also an Executor, ensure that you are clear in your letter of engagement that you are advising them in their capacity as Executor in connection with the administration of the estate and not as a beneficiary. There may be instances where you can act for a beneficiary as well as the Executor but it would serve you well to have a couple of contacts in other firms that you can refer the work onto in the event of a conflict. This will also help you maintain client relations as the beneficiary can be properly advised and is not cast adrift to try and find another solicitor who can act.

Managing Expectations

Once your client has been identified, you need to manage the expectations of the time it will take to wind up an estate. Depending on the client, this may well be your most difficult job. In Scotland, an estate should not be distributed before the 6 month anniversary of the death as this is the length of time creditors have to intimate debts. If an Executor distributes the estate prior to this time and then a new debt arises, the Executor can be personally liable to settle the debt. As a minimum, clients and beneficiaries should be advised that they will not receive any funds for 6 months after the death. In reality, it is more likely to take a year from instruction to wind up an estate and clients should be advised accordingly at the outset. This timeframe is likely to be extended if you have overseas assets, properties to be sold, businesses to be sold, where

---

5 This is usually a free of charge service where they confirm that the family tree matches the information you provided to them in the initial instruction. A charge usually only applies where your information does not match their information.

Inheritance Tax is due and the District Valuer becomes involved or where the Department of Work and Pensions launches an investigation into whether all assets were declared when any benefits claims were made during life.

Terms of Engagement

It goes without saying that your client should receive terms of engagement at the outset and the usual due diligence for anti-money laundering compliance undertaken.

Where you have multiple Executors, all of them need to engage with you at the outset before you can act on behalf of the Estate. Once you are instructed by all Executors, you can then act on instructions from a quorum of Executors.

Estates are tricky matters and what looks like a solvent estate on the initial meeting can quickly become insolvent as investigations into the extent of the estate get underway. Where this happens, it can often put full recovery of your fees in peril. Accordingly, consideration should be given as to whether your terms of engagement should include provision that in the event of insolvency the responsibility for paying fees should fall on the instructing party. Likewise, consider providing for the situation where the estate is solvent at the point of date of death but there are insufficient free proceeds to cover your fees or where it transpires the person instructing you does not have the title to act as Executor.

Another point to consider is how you record time against your file. If you do not have an all singing, all dancing electronic time recording system that can capture all time spent on your file, you may wish to consider the use of an independent law accountant to assess your fees. In this event, provision should be built into your terms of engagement to enable you to do so and for the law accountant's fee to be an authorised expense of the administration of the estate.

In addition, you may wish to consider whether you want to include a risk commission in your terms of engagement which includes an uplift in fees based on the value of the assets ingathered, for example, Bank and Building Societies balances 0.75%, insurance policies 1% etc.

Reporting a Death

Sometimes, you may find out about the death through a hospital or the police. This may be because the deceased was in hospital prior to their death and advised who to contact in the event of their death. It can also be because the police have found the body in the house and have searched the house and found a Will or correspondence with your details on it. Depending on who is appointed as Executor or what family members are available, you may also have to register the death.

You need to register the death within 8 days of the death (or when the body was found whichever is earlier) in Scotland including bank holidays and weekends. You will need details of the deceased's:

1. Name
2. Maiden surname (if applicable)
3. Marital status
4. Date of birth
5. Date of death
6. Place of death
7. Occupation
8. Last known address (if different from the place of death)
9. Parents names and occupations

You will also need the causes of the death which should be provided to you in the form of a medical certificate from the doctor certifying the death.

You may also need the deceased's national insurance number and proof of the above such as their passport, driving licence, a bill showing their address, birth, marriage or adoption certificates.

You will usually register the death at the Register of Births, Deaths and Marriages nearest to where the deceased died[6]. Any person who is over the age of 16 years old can register a death in Scotland although it is preferable that one of the following do so:

1. Any relative of the deceased;
2. Any person present when the person died;
3. The Executor or other legal representative; or
4. The occupier of the property where the person died

Extraordinary Registrations of Deaths

1. If the person has died in England and Wales, the death needs to be registered within 5 days of the death or the body being found. You can register the death if you:

    a. are a relative;

    b. were there at the time of death;

    c. are the person who found the body;

6 Search online for "Register a death" and the town of death to find the relevant registrar.

d. are the person in charge of a body;

e. are an administrator from the hospital (if the person died in hospital); or

f. are in charge of making funeral arrangements

2. If the person died in Northern Ireland, the death is registered via the District Registration Office and needs to be completed within 5 days. You can register the death if you:

   a. are a relative;

   b. were there at the time of death;

   c. are the person who found the body;

   d. are the person in charge of a body;

   e. are an administrator from the hospital (if the person died in hospital);

   f. are in charge of making funeral arrangements

   g. the governor, matron or chief officer of a public building where the death occurred; or

   h. a person living in and responsible for a house, lodgings or apartments where the death occurred; or

3. If the person died abroad, you must register the death according to the regulations of the country in which the person died. It is also possible to register the death in the United Kingdom in addition to the country of death but it is not necessary to do so. If the death is also registered in the UK, this will enable a Consular death certificate to be obtained and evidence of the death will readily be available through the National Records

Office of Scotland (or for registrations in Northern Ireland, England and Wales the General Register Offices).

4. If the person died on a foreign ship or aircraft, you must register the death in the country the ship or aircraft is registered in.

Funeral Arrangements and the right to dispose of a body

More often than not, the funeral will have been held or at the least instructed before the client comes to you to commence the administration of the estate. Your job in that case will simply be to ensure that the funeral is paid in the correct order of debts from the estate.

In most cases, there will be no argument over who makes the arrangements and it will be a case of "job done". However, there can be instances where the figurative all hell breaks loose over how the disposal of the deceased's body is to be arranged. Scots law has been relatively unclear on who has the right to dispose of a body. The Burial and Cremation (Scotland) Act 2016 sought to bring some clarity to the situation. Where an adult dies and does not leave what is known as an "arrangements on death declaration" the deceased's nearest relative can arrange for burial or cremation which for these purposes follows the following hierarchy[7]:

1. Spouse or civil partner8 ;

---

7 S65 Burial and Cremation (Scotland) Act 2016. Different provisions apply for the death of a child – see S66 Burial and Cremation (Scotland) Act 2016

8 unless they were formally separated or that person had deserted the deceased or the deceased has deserted them (S65(4)(a) Burial and Cremation (Scotland) Act 2016)

2. Cohabiting partner9;
3. Children (with step-children ranked equally here);
4. Parents of the deceased;
5. Siblings of the deceased;
6. Grandparents of the deceased;
7. Grandchildren of the deceased;
8. Aunts or uncles of the deceased;
9. Cousins of the deceased;
10. Nieces or nephews of the deceased;
11. A long-standing friend of the deceased can act where there is no one else who can qualify in one of the foregoing categories

An "arrangements on death declaration" means a declaration by the deceased specifying the person by whom the adult wishes the arrangements to be made for the burial or cremation of their remains on the adult's death. This can include a direction in a Will.

For the death of a minor, the nearest relative is defined as the parent(s) or person(s) having parental rights / responsibilities in relation to the child, followed by the child's siblings (if they are over 16), grandparents, and thereafter remoter relatives.

---

[9] where they couple were living together for at least six months before (i) the death or (ii) before the deceased was admitted to hospital if the deceased died there (S65(4)(b) Burial and Cremation (Scotland) Act 2016)

TIP – when writing Wills for clients and including provision for funeral instructions within the Will, ensure you advise your clients to tell their nearest and dearest their wishes for burial or cremation. It would not be the first time that a solicitor is notified about the death after the funeral has taken place only to discover on reading the Will that the deceased wished to be buried and had been cremated by the family. There is really not a lot that can be done to rectify that situation after the fact!

CHAPTER TWO

INTESTATE ESTATES

According to research, around 6 out of 10 adults in the UK don't have a Will[10]. Business development opportunities on the Will writing front aside, this means that more likely than not, you are going to have to administer an intestate estate (that is to say where the person died without leaving a Will) at some point in your career. In my experience, it also means that the estate is naturally going to cost more to administer as there are certain additional hoops that those connected to the estate are going to need to jump through to bring the estate to a close that would not be required had a Will been in place. An intestacy, in my experience, can expect to add 9–12 weeks as a minimum into the preliminary administration of the estate before you can obtain Confirmation.

Is a solicitor required?

The first question you should ask yourself is should you take on an intestate estate in the first place? The Sheriff Court local to where the deceased was domiciled can deal with the appointment of the Executor Dative and prepare the Confirmation application for free (although usual commissary fees apply) where the estate is classed as a small estate[11]. A small estate is currently where the total of the gross assets is less than £36,000[12]. A redirection of the prospect to the local Sheriff Court also dispenses with the need to obtain a Bond of Caution (pronounced "kay-

---

10 See www.unbiased.co.uk's 2015 article " UK's will-writing 'black holes' revealed by research for unbiased.co.uk's Write A Will Week"

11 Intestates Widows and Children (Scotland) Act 1875; Small Testate Estates (Scotland) Act 1876; Confirmation of Small Estates (Scotland) Act 1979 as amended

12 The Confirmation to Small Estates (Scotland) Order 2011 SSI 2011/435

shun") – a special type of insurance specific to Scotland which normally requires to be obtained when dealing with most intestate estates that require Confirmation. Please note that dispensing with the need to obtain a Bond of Caution where the Sheriff Court is preparing the paperwork only works if there is no competition for the role of Executor. Where there is competition for the role of Executor, a solicitor will need to become involved as the estate will likely involve an appearance in front of a Sheriff to resolve who out of the competing parties should be appointed as Executor (or in some cases, conjoin the appointment of Executors which is not without its own problems, particularly where the Executors do not get along!).

If you take on a small estate, you will need the Bond of Caution before you can apply for Confirmation which will add roughly 4-6 weeks onto the administration time with a starting insurance premium of around £270[13]. From a public relations point of view, directing a client to the Sheriff Court where there is a small estate could well gain you a substantial amount of good will and encourage the client to come back to you for further work on the basis that you appear to be one of the few and far between non money grabbing lawyers (since our profession seems to be tarred with that brush!). It will also help the prospect retain more of their inheritance as inevitably the administration fees for the administration of a small estate are disproportionately high percentage wise compared to the value of the estate.

Appointment of Executor

Where the estate cannot be dealt with via the Small Estates procedure, the first thing you will need to do is have an Executor Dative discerned. This will normally be the person with the closest degree of relationship to the deceased in terms of who is entitled to inherit[14]. It will come as no surprise that families do not always tell the truth about the extent of their

13 Starting premium from RSA as at November 2024

14 S2 Succession (Scotland) Act 1964

family and therefore when piecing together the family tree, it is always best to have it checked by a genealogist. Many offer a free checking service for your family tree. Details of genealogists are available at the useful addresses section of this book. It is also worth acknowledging that those left behind after the death may not be party to family secrets and therefore if there are additional children found or a child's sister is found to actually be their mother, it goes without saying that you need a large dose of diplomacy, empathy and tact when delivering news which will alter who is entitled to what from the estate. The delivery of such news may also alter the future relations between the various parties and not always for the better where affairs are revealed or someone finds out that who they thought their parents were are not in fact their biological parents.

The appointment of an Executor Dative is conducted by lodging an initial Writ with the Sheriff Court where the deceased was domiciled narrating the details of the death, the relatives the deceased was survived by along with those relatives who predeceased or divorced the deceased who would otherwise have preference to the party seeking appointment, confirmation that the petitioner is entitled to some or all of the estate and the capacity in which the petitioner should be discerned as Executor Dative eg as Executor Dative qua sister of the full blood of the deceased.

Styles for drafting the Initial Writ are outwith the scope of this book. Styles can however be found in "Currie on Confirmation" 9th Edition by Eilidh M Scobbie which is a fantastic resource for navigating even the most complex of drafting for the initial appointment of an Executor Dative.

Once lodged with the Sheriff Court, the details of the petition will be lodged on the Walls of Court. How long it will take for the details to appear on the Walls of Court will depend on how busy the courts are. Once 14 days have expired from the date that the details of the petition are lodged on the Walls of Court, if there are no objections, the petition will be granted. A copy of the interlocutor will thereafter (usually) be emailed to the solicitor thereafter. The current petition fee is £22[15].

Bond of Caution

Once you have your Executor or Executors appointed, you will need a Bond of Caution before you can proceed to obtain Confirmation to the estate. The only exception to this other than where the estate is a small estate is where the estate passes in full to the surviving spouse/civil partner[16].

A Bond of Caution is a special type of insurance designed to cover the situation whereby the Executor fails in his or her duty to administer the estate. It does not provide insurance for the Executor but rather is designed to protect beneficiaries and creditors of the estate. In effect, the Cautioner (the body providing the insurance) will guarantee the payments that should be made from the estate and will settle any due claims where the Executor has failed to do so. The Executor in turn will require to put the Cautioner back into the position that they would have been in had the Executor not failed in the exercise of their obligations.

Insurers for providing Bonds of Caution are few and far between in Scotland. There is a list of current providers at the back of this book under useful addresses but please check at the point of obtaining a Bond of Caution as insurers tend to come and go in Scotland for this type of insurance. There have been points in time where there has only been a single Caution provider.

---

15 As at November 2024. The fees change from time to time. Fees can be checked at www.scotcourts.gov.uk/ru les-and-practice/fees/sheriff-court-fees. Select "Commissary" for estate related fees.

16 Either where the deceased was not survived by any prior relatives under S77 Trusts and Succession (Scotland) Act 2024 or where the Spouse's prior rights exhaust the whole estate under S8-9 Succession (Scotland) Act 1964 as amended.

In order to apply for a Bond of Caution, you will need:

1. An irrevocable mandate from the Executor in favour of your firm to administer the estate;

2. A Bond of Caution signed by the Executor (which will in turn be counter signed by the insurer once the application has been approved);

3. A copy of the Confirmation application that will be submitted;

4. An application form narrating the details of the estate and the division of the same;

5. Copies of any deeds of variation, declinature of entitlement etc;

6. In the event that there is a Will, you will need to include a copy of the Will and explain why the estate requires a Bond of Caution[17]; and

7. Payment for the expected Bond of Caution fee

If you do not have ready cash within the estate at the point of applying for the Bond of Caution, ask your Executor to provide the funds. This should then be refunded to them out of the estate prior to any distributions being made to beneficiaries.

It will also normally be a condition of obtaining the Bond of Caution that you obtain clearance from the Department of Work and Pensions that there are no sums due to the estate. The easiest way to deal with this is to write to the debt management team of the Department of Work and

[17] For example, the Will may be invalid or you may have to have an Executor Dative appointed where there is a valid foreign Will with assets in Scotland but the Will does not appoint an Executor as the jurisdiction in which it was executed does not require such an appointment.

Pensions[18], advise of the estimated assets of the estate and ask them to confirm that no benefits have been overclaimed during life and whether any overpayments of properly claimed benefits have occurred which will need to be repaid by the estate (if any).

Division of the Estate

The division of an intestate estate follows the division rules set out in the Succession (Scotland) Act 1964 as amended and the Trusts and Succession (Scotland) Act 2024 and are as follows:

1. 100% to the spouse/civil partner where the prior rights of a spouse/civil partner[19] exhaust the whole estate OR where the deceased is survived by a spouse/civil partner but no issue[20];

2. Where a spouse/civil partner is not entitled to take the whole estate, the prior rights of the spouse take first priority then the spouse/civil partner is entitled to legal rights in the remaining moveable estate which will equate to one half where there are no children, and one third where there are children of the deceased. Thereafter if there are children of the deceased (or remoter descendants in the case of a predeceasing child), the remainder of the estate passes to the children or their issue in the case of a predeceasing child to the exclusion of the spouse/civil partner.

---

18 Department for Work and Pensions, Recovery from Estates (Scotland), Debt Management (RES), Mail Handling Site A, Wolverhampton, WV98 2DH

19 S8-9 Succession (Scotland) Act 1964 as amended.

20 S77 Trusts and Succession (Scotland) Act 2024 for deaths on or after 30 April 2024.

3. Where there are no children nor a surviving spouse/civil partner, the estate passes to the parents/siblings of the deceased with representation by issue.

4. Where there are no children or remoter descendants, siblings or remoter descendants, parents or spouse/civil partner to inherit, succession to the estate follows the family tree up the way branch by branch until a generation is located to inherit the estate;

5. If there are no living family members to be found, the estate passes to the Crown as *ultimus haeres.*

If you suspect that there will be no family of the deceased to be located, contact the National Ultimus Haeres unit[21] as soon as possible for guidance on whether you should continue to act.

Confirmation

Once the Bond of Caution has been obtained, this is then lodged with the application for Confirmation and the remainder of the estate is administered as usual.

Disengagement

Please note that unlike any other piece of work you may take on for a client, where there has been a Bond of Caution issued, the client cannot simply decide to un-instruct you. Where the client is unhappy with your handling of the estate or a conflict arises that requires you to disengage, the client will need to instruct another solicitor to continue acting and the Cautioner will need to be advised and consent to the change in representation otherwise the Executor can find themselves in breach of the terms of the Bond.

---

21 The National Ultimus Haeres Unit, Procurator Fiscal Office, Cameronian House, 3/5 Almada Street, Hamilton, ML3 0HG

CHAPTER THREE

TESTATE ESTATES

A testate Estate is one in which there is a valid Will. The Will normally appoint Executors, provide details of any legacies and deals with the division of the residue of the estate. It may on occasion provide details of the manner in which the body should be disposed of and provide details of who should act as guardians for minor children as well as any specific powers of the Executors.

Locating the Will

The Will can – usually – be located with the solicitor who drafted the Will. In this situation, most people will have a letter from their solicitor with a copy of the Will among their personal papers that will lead you to the firm that holds the Will. If the firm no longer exists, you can contact the Interventions team at the Law Society of Scotland[22] and they will advise who took over the safe keeping for the firm. This may lead you into a little bit of a detective work if the firm in question has been taken over multiple times before you can locate the Will.

Of course, a solicitor is not required to make a Will. Anyone can make a Will from age 12 in Scotland. If the whereabouts of a Will is not immediately apparent, a thorough search of the deceased's property should be undertaken to ascertain if the Will is in the house or otherwise if there is information which may lead to the Will being located elsewhere. While not a common service now, it used to be the case that banks had safe keeping vaults which customers could use. If you cannot locate a Will, it is always worth checking with the deceased's bank to see if they hold the Will (or indeed anything else) on behalf of the deceased.

---

[22] Interventions@lawscot.org.uk

If a person has had a conversation with the now deceased testator in which they advised that they had made a Will but did not disclose who made the Will or where it is stored, you can place an advert in the Law Society of Scotland Journal detailing the name of the deceased and any other personal information such as last known address and date of birth. This will enable other solicitors to check their records in case they hold the Will.

An alternative to the advert is if you know the approximate geographical area of where the person would have been at the time the purported Will was made would be to write to the solicitors in that area to enquire if they held a Will. Depending on the area and popularity of law firm businesses, this may involve a handful of letters/emails or may involve several hundred if a major city is involved. The costs involved in conducting such a search should be weighed up against the potential for a disappointed beneficiary who may be excluded from benefiting in the event that a Will cannot be located.

You may also wish to check with the Certainty Will Register[23] to ascertain if they hold details of the Will. This is mainly used to register the locations of English Wills but has been used by some Scottish law firms and will writing companies too. The Certainty Will Register doesn't hold the actual Will but holds details of where a Will is held. It is supposed to act like a central register of Wills so that Wills can be found and enacted with ease.

The Royal Faculty of Procurators Library[24] in Glasgow also offers a search facility in which it will send out an email to its members to try and locate Wills of deceased people.

23 www.nationalwillregister.co.uk

24 www.rfpg.org

Validity of Will

In order to be a self-proving valid Will that can be admitted into the Confirmation process, the testamentary document needs to meet the following criteria:

1. Designate a testator – that is to say, the person granting the Will

2. It must be signed on every page by the Testator or his representative[25]

3. It should also be witnessed on the last page by one witness who is over the age of 16 years old and who is not named in the Will[26]

---

25 Under the Requirements of Writing (Scotland) Act 1995, the only representative who can sign on behalf of a testator who retains mental capacity is a Notary Public. This would be in circumstances whereby, for example, the testator is unable to write due to physical frailty or where the testator is blind. A notarial executed Will will be self-proving if it meets all of the rest of the criteria for a valid Will. The procedure for undertaking a notarial execution of a Will is set out at S9(3) and Schedule 3 of the Requirements of Writing (Scotland) Act 1995. Guidance on the requirements for a notarial execution of a Will can be found at https://www.lawscot.org.uk/members/rules-and-guidance/rules-and-guidance/section-f/division-e/guidance/guidance-re-acting-as-a-notary-public. It is also possible for the Court to sanction a representative to sign a testamentary writing on behalf of an incapax person through an intervention order or guardianship order however it must be proved that to do so would be in the best interests of the incapax adult. See T Applicant, 2005 SLT (Sh Ct) 97

26 Requirements of Writing (Scotland) Act 1995. Wills executed prior to 1st August 1995 require two people to act as witnesses to the signature of the testator.

4. The testator must have had capacity to enter into the Will[27]

The first stage when looking at a Will is to check that the Will is signed on every page and witnessed on the last page.

The next stage is to check that there is a completed testing clause. If the testing clause has not been completed but it has otherwise been validly signed by the Testator, the testing clause can be added post death providing that the Will has not been admitted to Confirmation or registered with the Books of Council and Session. You might rightfully wonder where you might get the information to do so in this scenario. If Wills are being sent out to be signed to the client, the firm might send a separate signing schedule to be completed with the details of the witness and the date and place of signing to enable the law firm to complete the testing clause upon return. This may be stored with the Will and can be used to complete the testing clause. Otherwise file notes from a meeting or telephone call may be capable of being used to complete the details of the testing clause.

Keeping the Will safe

It goes without saying that you need to keep the Will safe to administer the estate as it will be required to obtain Confirmation to the estate. It should either be kept in the strong room at your firm or alternatively it can be sent to the Books of Council and Session to be registered post death. You will then receive an extract of the Will which can be admitted to Confirmation in place of the original Will. Ideally when sending a

---

[27] S2(2) Age of Legal Capacity (Scotland) Act 1991 provides that a person has testamentary capacity from age 12. It is also worth looking at the English case of Banks v. Goodfellow 1870. LR 5 QB 549 which has a really good commentary on what to look out for when dealing with testamentary capacity. Its principals are not enshrined in Scots law but in my personal opinion, if you follow the rules in the case, it will help assist with keeping a claim from your door when making a Will for someone with mental health issues.

principal Will anywhere, it should be sent by some form of tracked delivery in order that should it go missing, you can establish in Court at what point it went missing and who was the last person to have it.

TOP TIP – manage risk when writing Wills. You should as a matter of course have a checklist when preparing the Will to ensure that it contains no mistakes. In particular look at clause numbering as depending on whether you free hand draft, work from styes or have a case management system that helps produce your Will, if you are adding or removing clauses this is where clause numbering can go awry. Also make sure that there are at least some words from your final paragraph attached to your testing clause. Equally, you should have a check list for the Will after execution to make sure the Will is formally valid before it is stored in your safe keeping facility.

Non-compliant Wills

If a document does not meet all of the above criteria, it does not mean that the Will is not valid – it is just not self-proving. This means that an additional court process will be required to have the Will admitted into the Confirmation process.

The process of setting up the Will involves persuading a Sheriff that a document purporting to be the last Will of the deceased should be admitted to Confirmation. This will require affidavits from those who can attest to what happened in the creation of the Will and general evidence from those that that the Testator may have told regarding their testamentary intentions. As you might anticipate, this is not a quick or cheap process and therefore testamentary writings should be checked as soon as possible to ascertain if a court process will be required in connection with the administration of the estate.

Missing Wills

In the case of a lost or accidentally destroyed Will, a copy can be admitted to Court for Confirmation. This is known as Proving the Tenor of a Will.

Where a copy is being requested to be admitted to Confirmation, this will require affidavits from those who can attest to the circumstances of loss as well as from the witness or witnesses named in the Will who can attest to a Will being executed by the deceased.

Usually, where the circumstances are straight forward, the Sheriff will grant the motion on the basis of affidavit evidence. If, however, there is a conflict in the evidence or an objection to the motion (for example from a beneficiary who would inherit more under intestacy than they would if the Will was admitted to Confirmation) then an appearance will more than likely be required to resolve the issue of the Will.

If you become involved in the need to prove the tenor of a Will, expect it to add around 3-6 months as a minimum in administration time as well as several thousand pounds in additional expense and outlays. It is therefore really important that you have a really tight process in place for maintaining safekeeping to avoid Wills going missing in your firm.

Missing Will V Intestacy

Where the original Will is missing and the terms of the Will mirror the distribution according to the laws of intestacy, you may be tempted to take a practical view and simply deal with the estate under intestate procedure. After all, the same outcome is achieved and it will likely be significantly cheaper than having to deal with the court process to have a copy of the Will admitted into Confirmation. The Professional Practices division of the Law Society of Scotland take a different view[28] and advise that where a copy Will is available, proving the tenor would be the appropriate course of action. The reasoning behind this is in connection with Executors declaration on the C1 form (application for Confirmation) concerning knowledge of any testamentary writings that are not included with application. While the C1 forms have changed

[28] https://www.lawscot.org.uk/members/journal/issues/vol-63-issue-12/lost-will-what-then/

since the guidance from the Law Society was issued, the Executors still require to declare that they do not know of any testamentary settlement or writing relating to the disposal of the deceased's estate or any part of the deceased's estate other than those referred to in the declaration. Therefore having an Executor sign such a declaration on intestacy in the knowledge that there was a Will but it cannot be located would be fundamentally unacceptable.

CHAPTER FOUR

STARTING THE ADMINISTRATION OF THE ESTATE

Documents you will need

In order to administer the estate, you will need as bare minimum a full extract death certificate for the deceased. On registration of the death, the person registering the death will be provided with the abbreviated death certificate free of charge. It will be necessary to pay to obtain at least one full extract. Where it is a large estate or there are multiple life policies, it would be wise to obtain a couple of copies of the full death certificate to speed up the circulation of documents to asset holders. Otherwise, you may need to wait for the original death certificate to be returned from the first asset holder before you can make enquiries to establish the extent of the estate with other asset holders.

If no full extract death certificate was obtained or if further copies are required, these can be obtained from the Register of Births, Deaths and Marriages for the council in which the deceased died. You can also – usually – order copies online at www.scotlandspeople.gov.uk. This website is particularly useful where you need to locate death certificates for historic deaths eg to prove that a house has passed on survivorship to your deceased on the death of their late spouse some years prior.

Where it is a testate estate, you will also need the original Will and any Codicils and informal writings.

Other documents concerning the deceased which would be useful to have include:

1. Birth certificate
2. Adoption certificate
3. Marriage certificate
4. Separation agreement
5. Decrees of Divorce
6. Passport
7. Driving licence
8. HMRC statement (which may not be available if the deceased had not previously been in the self-assessment regime)
9. Statement of benefits letter from the Department of Work and Pensions
10. National insurance number

Thereafter, you need to ascertain the extent of the estate. That means locating all of the deceased's assets and ascertaining the extent of their funeral expenses and debts.

<u>Why do you need to locate the assets?</u>

The Grant of Confirmation in Scotland includes an inventory of each individual asset held by the deceased. You will then usually obtain a certificate of Confirmation for each asset that specifies the details of the asset along with details of the Executors and will contain a court seal. The Certificate is then sent to the asset holder as authority that they can act on the instructions of the Executors to sell or transfer the assets. You can of course order multiple copies of the Confirmation booklet which can also do the same thing but this costs more than the certificates will[29]. In general, unless the asset is of minimal value, the asset holder will require sight of Confirmation narrating the asset in question (which for these purposes will be either the Confirmation Booklet or the relevant Certificate for the individual asset). It is for this reason that it is important that all assets are identified prior to applying for Confirmation.

In addition, the inventory forms the basis for assessing whether there is Inheritance Tax due on the estate. It is therefore important that the assets and debts are ascertained as soon as possible in order to calculate the amount of Inheritance Tax due (if any) on the estate and ensure that the Executor makes as truthful a declaration on the extent of the estate assets and the Inheritance Tax due as possible.

Worst case scenario that you miss an asset (for example, because it has been sitting as a dormant account with a bank and no correspondence was found among the deceased's papers which would lead you to contact the bank in the first instance or because the asset holder does not tell you about any other assets the deceased held outwith those you have contacted them about), you can always apply for an Eik (pronounced "eeek" – like the noise you might make if you see a mouse in your house!) to Confirmation which will enable you to obtain the required Confirmation for the asset. The downside to this is that needing to apply for an Eik will incur additional court and legal fees which may be substantial depending on the value of the assets which were omitted from the original application for Confirmation.

In addition, the inventory of the estate will form the basis for the calculation of any legal rights claims which apply to the estate. It is

29 From 1 November 2024, certificates are £9 each whereas copy Confirmation booklets are £14 if ordered at the time of applying for Confirmation or £32 for the first copy and £14 thereafter for any requests made after the initial application – see https://www.scotcourts.gov.uk/taking-action/court-fees/sheriff-court-fees/ for further information on commissary fees. The fees change periodically so do check before applying.

therefore extremely important to ensure that the value of the assets is correct to avoid over or understating the extent of the claims for legal rights (for further information see Chapter Eleven of this book).

Turning Detective – Finding the deceased's assets and debts

If you are lucky, the deceased will have been super organised and you will be able to collect their box of papers with details of all their assets and the location of important papers from the bottom of their wardrobe or other safe place. More likely than not, you are going to have to get your detective cap on and go digging to ascertain the extent of the assets and debts.

It used to be the case that you could put a 6–12 months redirection of mail on the deceased's residence and you could be reasonably certain you would have caught all potential assets and debts. While a mail redirection should still be organised where the property is now unoccupied, as more and more people manage their banking and investments online, it is becoming increasingly difficult to locate assets and debts where there is not a traditional paper trail.

Paper documents will always be your starting point. If you are tasked with trying to locate papers (for example, because the family are uncertain that they have found everything or where one or more of your solicitors or your trust company is appointed as Executor) you will need to thoroughly search the deceased's property to ensure you have located any papers relaying to potential assets and debts of the deceased. You may wish to consider whether a colleague should accompany you to the deceased's property for three reasons:

1. For personal safety;

2. To speed up the search process – many hands make light work; and

3. In case any money is found or there are items of significant value in the property such as jewellery.

Before you take any offence, I am not considering any skulduggery on your part by suggesting you take a colleague with you! This is simply to cover you in the event a family member or friend suggests there was cash or other valuables in the property and you either can't find them or don't find as much as expected and you are then in the hot seat as prime suspect no 1! It also covers you in the hopefully unlikely event that you were to be mugged en route to your firm's bank with cash from the property as there will be a witness to the incident. It also prevents the situation arising whereby you find yourself alone in a property with someone who exhibits behaviour which would indicate that you would not wish to be on your own with them.

People stash details of their assets (and indeed their cash!) in the most unlikely of places so on a house visit search everywhere… and I mean everywhere! The usual suspect places for cash and assets are wardrobes, drawers, cupboards, under beds and desks. Coat pockets and bags are also a likely source of bank cards and cash. Some of the more unusual places where I have found documents and cash are in the freezer, the biscuit tin, in pots in the cupboard, behind paintings and in the cistern! (I wish I could take credit for the genius of looking in the cistern but alas, it was a house clearing company that I had booked to attend who suggested it as a place they had found cash previously and lo and behold we found some in a plastic bag taped to the inside of the lid!). Under floor boards is another place to look – now I am not suggesting that you take a crow bar with you on a home visit to rip up every floor board in sight on the off chance that you find a secret stash but if you find yourself walking across a particularly squeaky board near the edge of a carpet, it may just be worthwhile having a peek.

You should also look in wallets and purses to find cash, membership, loyalty scheme and bank cards. Unused gift cards and loyalty scheme vouchers/accrued points can also have a value.

Things to look out for when searching a house

In addition to looking for details of assets and debts, there are some other things that you should look out for to secure the deceased's estate.

Passport

Not strictly speaking an asset but should you come across passports for the deceased – expired or current – these should be sent to the Passport Office for cancellation. You should ask the family whether these should be returned as the Passport Office is happy to do so but will destroy them if not otherwise instructed. The reason for cancellation of passports is to prevent identity theft. You should also keep a copy of the passport in your file in case you need to provide proof of signature of the deceased to link assets to them or you require proof of their signature. The passport can also be cancelled through the "Tell us once" service , details of which will be provided to the person registering the death. The service enables all relevant government agencies to be told about the death in a single application.

Driving licence

Much like passports, notifying the DVLA about the death isn't about finding assets as such but about prevention of identity theft. You should however ask the DVLA to check if there are any vehicles registered in the deceased's name that you have not otherwise found out about.

Vehicles

You will need the V5 for any vehicles owned by the deceased before you can sell or transfer the vehicle. The log book would also be useful to locate particularly if the vehicle is to be sold to obtain the highest possible price. This may be in the house but can often be found in the glove box or in or under the boot of the car.

Bank/Credit Cards

When dealing with bank and credit cards, cut the cards in two or more pieces to ensure they cannot be used. This is particularly important now with the advent of contactless technologies to prevent them being used post death inappropriately, particularly if they are being posted back to the bank.

Likewise, if you come across a cheque book, you should cancel each unused cheque to prevent encashment. For those readers who are lucky enough to be too young to remember how this should be done, put two diagonal lines across each blank cheque and write "cancelled" in between the two lines.

Honours

Receipt of Honours such as OBE, CBE, MBE etc are more common than you might expect. If you find an award among the deceased's personal effects or are otherwise told that they held an Honour, you will need to advise The Chancery at St James Palace. While I have yet to have a request from the Chancery to return an award, it is a question I usually ask on notification of the death to ensure the award ends up in the right place. I also normally ask if The Chancery has any additional obligations that the Executors need to comply with. The staff at The Chancery are extremely helpful at navigating you through what needs to be done in respect of each award.

Share Certificates

If you find share certificates (they do still exist even with the popularity of Discretionary Fund Managers!), take them back to the office and put in your safe until you can establish which ones are valid. You will need these to sell or transfer the shares.

Life Policies/Investment Bond documentation

If you find life policy certificates/schedules and/or Investment Bond documentation, take these back to the office with you as they may be required to make a claim following the death.

Insurance certificates

This can be for home insurance as well as life and/or accident insurance. Keep these safe as they may need to be produced to make a claim.

Secure valuables

If there are any valuables in the property such as jewellery, you may wish to take these back to the office to put in your safe or where they are to be sold, consider consigning them to an auction house for safe keeping.

Property

While title deeds can likely be found with a mortgage provider or a solicitor, sometime they can be located within the property so it is worthwhile looking to see if you can find them or otherwise details of who may hold them so you can obtain them during the administration of the estate. If the titles cannot be located anywhere, you should be able to download a copy of the titles from either the Sasines Register or Land Register at the Registers of Scotland. This is not without a cost to the estate however so if you do find these documents in the property, you should take them with you back to the office.

Changing the locks

You may wish to consider whether you wish to change the locks to the property particularly where the property is unoccupied following the death or where there is a family fall out over who is getting what from the house. This means you have complete control over who enters the property and in the case of a fall out between family members / beneficiaries / people who think they should be entitled to certain things but are not, means that assets should not simply "disappear" without your consent.

CHAPTER FIVE

INITIAL INVESTIGATIONS

Once you believe you have located all of the information concerning the deceased's possible assets and debts and secured any vehicles and property, you need to commence with the initial investigations.

Depending on the nature of the possible assets and debts and how quick asset holders respond, this stage is likely to take around 12-16 weeks to complete. This timeframe is likely to be significantly extended if you have foreign assets that need to be identified or if there is a business involved.

You will need to contact every potential asset holder and creditor to assess the extent of the asset/debt at the date of death. The assessment should always be on the basis of an open market valuation between a willing buyer and seller. Unlike insurance valuations, the valuation is undertaken on the price that a willing buyer would be prepared to buy the asset in its current condition rather than on a new for old valuation basis.

Property and land

Where the estate is not subject to Inheritance Tax, an estimated value for property and/or land can be used for Confirmation purposes. This could be from an estate agent or from an online portal which provides estimates of house prices[30].

Where the estate is likely to or is going to be subject to Inheritance Tax or in circumstances where the market is on a rapid upward trajectory and capital gains tax on disposal is likely to be an issue, you should obtain a formal valuation of the property and/or land from a surveyor. If the property and/or land is also likely to be sold, you may wish to ask the

[30] See for example, https://www.zoopla.co.uk/house-prices/

surveyor if they offer a discount for undertaking both the Inheritance Tax valuation and the home report where there is a residential property involved as certain surveyors will offer a package. Do not however instruct the home report until you are ready to market the property as home reports have a limited shelf life and will otherwise need to be refreshed at a cost to the estate at least once if you undertake it too early.

When instructing the survey, you need to advise the surveyor that it is a survey for Inheritance Tax purposes and that it should be for an open market value on the date of death between a willing buyer and seller. You also need to advise the surveyor to take account of any development potential for the property and/or land as this is also subject to Inheritance Tax.

You might also wish to ask the surveyor for a reinstatement valuation for insurance purposes to make sure your Executors have sufficiently insured the building in the event that a claim requires to be made. You should also alert the surveyor to any damage to the property that happened prior to the death that had not been fixed at the time of the survey or damage that occurred after the death but before the survey was undertaken.

TOP TIP – make sure your letter of engagement makes it clear that the obligation to insure the property rests with the Executors and not with your firm. You should also make it clear that you will not be responsible for reminding the Executors about renewal dates falling due. You do not want to be in the position whereby your firm could be on the hook for failing to insure a property if a claim is made.

If there is any disagreement between the Executors, beneficiaries or indeed your own professional view on the figure which is returned from the valuer, you may wish to consider instructing a second valuation on the same terms to corroborate the value provided. If nothing else, your Executors will be able to demonstrate that they have taken all reasonable steps to verify the value of the property in the event of a query from the District Valuer. Of course, this could lead to the situation whereby the valuers disagree on the value to be used. Where the values differ significantly, you may need to instruct a third valuation to identify and set aside the errant value. In any event, your surveyor should be able to discuss with you their reasoning for the value they have attributed to your property.

Crofts

These are parcels of land which are specific to Scotland and have danger written all over them! Where there is a croft involved in an estate, you will need to ascertain what type of croft you are dealing with as this will determine how you proceed with dealing with the croft later in the administration. In any event you will need to have the croft or the tenancy thereof valued at the date of death.

The types of crofts are as follows:

Owner occupied croft – this is a type of croft whereby the person is the owner of a croft, was the crofter of the land at the time it was acquired or acquired title as the nominee of the crofter or otherwise through succession laws or purchased the croft from the landlord and a new croft was created and that the croft has not been let out as a croft by the owner.

Croft tenancy – the asset here is the tenancy rather than the land and buildings itself which can in some instances be highly valuable. The tenancy may be of land or land plus buildings. The deceased will either be the tenant or the landlord (although the Landlord is more often than not likely to be either the Scottish government or a landed Estate).

Decrofted land – land and/or buildings which were previously subject to crofting law but have been taken out of the crofting law remit by a voluntary process. This land is treated like any other land and/or property with no special procedures required.

In addition to narrating the extent of the tenancy and/or the land and buildings, you will also need to identify whether there are any livestock included (referred to as a souming) which needs to be included in the

Confirmation application. This can be identified from either the Crofting Register[31] or the Register of Crofts[32] depending on where the croft is registered.

Where there is a testate estate, you have 12 months from the date of death to transfer the croft tenancy to the beneficiary. Where there is an intestate estate, this timeframe is extended to 24 months. If the deadline is missed, you will need to obtain agreement from the Landlord to extend the timeframe. Please note that an extension to the time frame is not automatic and therefore estates involving crofts should be expeditated as much as possible to avoid falling foul of the timescales. If the transfer takes too long, the tenancy can be marketed by the Crofting Commission. It is however possible to have such marketing put on hold where you can prove that the administration of the estate is moving although it is by no means guaranteed that the Commission will agree to it.

A point to note is that if there is a crofting tenancy in a testate estate it can only be bequeathed to a single individual or two or more individuals where each has a right to the whole tenancy and no part of the croft would become untenanted as a result of the bequest. Where this gets tricky is where a testator tries to split a croft in a Will e.g. a field to his son and the house to his daughter. As crofted tenancy law is a particularly difficult area of law to navigate, it is worth getting an independent opinion from a crofting specialist to make sure that any bequests are valid and to confirm who is entitled to it in the event that the bequest in the Will is found to be invalid. This is not the case with owner occupied crofts which can be bequeathed to any number of people who would all become joint owners.

31 https://www.crofts.ros.gov.uk/register/search

32 https://www.crofting.scotland.gov.uk/register-of-crofts

Where there are livestock involved, you will need to obtain a valuation for them as well as any farming equipment which is not otherwise contained in the valuation of the crofting business.

A practical pointer for crofts involving livestock (and indeed for farms) is to make sure they are being looked after or otherwise sold off at the earliest possible opportunity. The last thing you need to be dealing with during the administration of the estate is the disposal of dead animals!

Farm and Agricultural Land

When dealing with farm and agricultural land, you will need to establish whether the land is owned (either by the deceased or through a business such as a farming partnership) or tenanted. Like any other property, it will need to be valued at the date of death. If the land or tenancy is held by a business, the value of the land or tenancy will form part of the valuation of the business.

Like crofts, tenanted farm and agricultural lands are a potential source of danger to the administration of an estate. There are different types of tenancies that can apply depending under which act the tenancy was created[33]. Where you have a tenancy, the terms of the lease will need to be checked to see whether there is prohibition against the tenant being able to bequeath the lease to another person.

There are also only certain people who can inherit the tenancy as follows[34]:

1. Any person who would be, or would in any circumstances have been, entitled to succeed to the tenant's estate on intestacy by virtue of the Succession (Scotland) Act 1964;

[33] Agricultural Holdings (Scotland) Act 1991 and Agricultural Holdings (Scotland) Act 2003

[34] S11 Agricultural Holdings (Scotland) Act 1991 as amended

2. A spouse or civil partner of a child of the tenant;
3. A spouse or civil partner of a grandchild of the tenant;
4. A spouse or civil partner of a brother or sister of the tenant;
5. A brother or sister of the tenant's spouse or civil partner;
6. A spouse or civil partner of such a brother or sister;
7. A child (including a step-child) of such a brother or sister;
8. A grandchild (including a step-grandchild) of such a brother or sister;
9. A step-child of the tenant;
10. A spouse or civil partner of such a step-child;
11. A descendant of such a step-child;
12. A step-brother or step-sister of the tenant;
13. A spouse or civil partner of such a step-brother or step-sister; or
14. A descendant of such a step-brother or step-sister.

The recipient of the bequest of the tenancy has 21 days from the date of death to intimate acceptance of the bequest to the landlord[35]. Given that people will often let the funeral pass before instructing a solicitor to deal with the administration of the estate, you will appreciate that 3 weeks after the date of death is not a long time at all for a person to understand they have been left a tenancy and accept the bequest.

---

35 S12 Agricultural Holdings (Scotland) Act 1991 as amended

If the Lease prohibits the tenant from leaving his interest as tenant in his Will, or if the tenant dies intestate, Confirmation to the tenancy should be obtained and the tenancy transferred to an appropriate person within one year of the death. Thereafter the recipient has 21 days from the date of transfer to intimate receipt of the tenancy.

Failure to comply with timescales can see the tenancy lost. The landlord can object to a transfer so even if you do comply with the timescales, the transfer is by no means guaranteed.

Also a word of caution when dealing with these types of assets – if the land/buildings form part of the business, the nature of the asset can change from heritable to moveable which can significantly inflate the value of any legal rights claims on the estate.

Timeshares

Timeshares are, in short, a nightmare, particularly if you happen to have a foreign one. They are difficult to value and they are difficult to dispose of. The timeshare provider should be able to provide you with a value for the timeshare. If you are dealing with a reputable timeshare provider, your Executor may need to pay a fee to sell or transfer the timeshare. If your deceased had the misfortune to be involved with a less than reputable time share provider, you may well find yourself stuck in a cycle of trying to get the timeshare sold or transferred and may well find that the cost of doing so outweighs the benefit to the estate. In such circumstances, it may be necessary to attempt to renounce entitlement to the timeshare.

Personal Effects

For inheritance tax purposes, personal effects are valued on an old for old basis. Essentially, what this means is what a willing buyer would be prepared to pay for the items in their current condition in open market conditions. This is different to an insurance valuation which would provide cover for a new replacement.

For a significant part of the population, the deceased will only have what can be deemed as regular personal effects, for example, beds, wardrobes, sofas, pots and pans etc. Many household items will no longer meet current health and safety standards and will therefore be unsellable and attract a nil value for these purposes.

Again, if inheritance tax is likely or going to be an issue, you should have the contents professionally valued. Most auction houses offer this service. The valuation should be stated to be assessed as at the date of death. It is not uncommon for a nil or nominal value to be attributed to the value of the personal effects by a valuer where the deceased had only what might be deemed to be regular household contents, particularly for properties which have been in need of substantial modernisation where the contents do not meet current fire retardancy standards. You may well find that the cost of the valuation may be more than the contents themselves that are valued in the latter scenario.

You will also wish to consider whether personal effects should be formally valued if there are potential legal rights claim on the estate as the personal effects will form part of that calculation. An estimated value may be acceptable where family relations are amicable or a beneficiary may insist upon having a valuation undertaken. If using an estimated valuation for legal rights calculations, you should advise the claimants that an estimated value has been used to minimise costs to the estate and that they are able to request a formal valuation to confirm the final value used. If a valuation is requested, it goes without saying that the claimant may receive more or less than they would have done with the estimated valuation.

If the deceased had any collections such as stamps, coins, crystal, Wedgewood plates etc, these should be valued by an appropriate valuer. If an auction house is unable to value them for whatever reason, they should be able to provide details of appropriate valuers.

Vehicles

You can use either a valuation for the vehicle such as from Parkers[36] or Glass[37] or you can use a sold valuation if the car is sold between the death and obtaining Confirmation (assuming the sold price is representative of the value that would have been obtained at the date of death).

If you cannot locate the V5 for any vehicles owned by the deceased, you will need to contact the DVLA for a replacement before the vehicle can be sold or transferred. You will also need to check the MOT[38] and taxation status[39] of the vehicle to ensure that the vehicle does not get impounded for being illegal on either front. If the car is being maintained on private land and is not on the road, the Executor's can request a SORN which will prevent tax having to be paid.

TOP TIP – make sure your letter of engagement makes it clear that the obligation to insure the car, tax it and maintain an up-to-date MOT rests with the Executors and not with your firm. You should also make it clear that you will not be responsible for reminding the Executors about renewal dates falling due. You do not want to be in the position whereby your firm could be on the hook for failures in this respect, particularly if someone drives the car uninsured.

Also check the ownership status of the car in terms of whether it remains under the terms of a finance agreement. You will normally find details of a lender among the direct debits on the deceased's bank account if you cannot locate any paperwork to confirm one way or another within the deceased's papers. If the car is on hire purchase, the vehicle does not belong to the deceased and therefore the Executors will have a decision

36 https://www.parkers.co.uk/

37 https://glass.co.uk

38 https://www.gov.uk/check-mot-status

39 https://www.gov.uk/check-vehicle-tax

to make about paying off the balance and retaining the asset or handing back the keys and reducing the extent of the debt.

Registration Plate

Believe it or not, some registration plates for vehicles can have a value separate from the vehicle it is registered to which can run from a few hundred pounds to eight figures. The world's most expensive registration plate was held in Dubai and sold for an eye watering £12m[40]. Registration marks which accrue value are usually private registration marks. A value can be obtained from a car or plate dealership.

Caravans – static and mobile

Caravans will vary in value and usually the caravan park upon which it is parked will be able to provide a valuation. One thing to bear in mind with caravans that are on a caravan park is that on site fees will continue to accrue. The estate may also be subject to winter storage charges and transfer of pitch charges going forward.

In addition, if the site does not allow the caravan to stay on site over winter or does not offer over winter storage, your Executors may have to look at obtaining off site storage and arranging transport for the same.

Yachts, Boats, Ships and Aircraft

Like a vehicle, boats and aircraft will need to be valued for Inheritance Tax purposes. This is not an exact science (much like cars) as the value will depend on how well they have been maintained. Contact a broker for a value who may well send out a surveyor to confirm the estimated value. As with any other asset, the true value of the asset will only be discovered when it is placed on the open market.

---

[40] The plate P7 was sold in the UAE in 2023.

For the purposes of where the asset is placed on the Confirmation document, the boat or aircraft will fall under the jurisdiction of the country in which it is registered

One thing you will need to make sure you do is make arrangements to keep the boat berthed or the aircraft standing while the administration of the estate is undertaken. You may be able to negotiate payment of fees to be paid post Confirmation or where there are no funds in the estate, the Executors may need to make other financial arrangements to meet the costs (which may include a loan or a beneficiary taking over responsibility who can be reimbursed from the estate at a later date).

Bank/Building Society Accounts

You will need to ascertain the capital balance on the account and any interest accrued but not yet paid at the date of death.

With increasing use of paperless statements, you may need to rely on the deceased's bank/building society card(s) to ascertain which bank or building society the deceased had accounts with. Not all bank cards will have an account number printed on them. If you haven't found statements in the house for the bank or building society and the card doesn't have an account number, I normally attach the cut-up cards to the letter with sticky tape to help the bank locate the deceased's accounts. I also usually ask whether the deceased held any other products with them other than the ones that have been intimated, either in the deceased's name or held jointly with another.

You will also find that more and more banks and building societies are shunning the traditional way of intimating a death in favour of online portals. Details of some of the portals are at the useful addresses section of this book.

When contacting a bank for details of the assets, you should also ask them to provide details of an interest paid during the current and previous tax year in order that you can ascertain the extent of any tax that the deceased owed or was due to be refunded by HMRC.

In addition, you should ask for details of all standing orders and direct debits on the accounts. This will give you leads for other assets which you may not have found paperwork for as well as most likely details of who the deceased was indebted too as well as the basics like who supplies the utilities for the deceased.

You should also ask whether the bank or building society is holding anything in safe custody for the deceased. Banks in particular frequently used to offer a safe custody service and you may find other assets or important papers in their vaults.

Business Interests

A business interest for the deceased will take the form of the deceased being a sole trader, being a partner in a partnership or owning shares in a company.

The starting point for valuing the business will be the deceased's accountant. Where the deceased has been a sole trader or a partner, it will be necessary for the books to be brought up to the date of date of death to establish the date of death value.

Unless a partnership agreement provides otherwise, on the death of a partner, the partnership is dissolved and wound up with the net assets (or liabilities) shared between the partners and the deceased partner's estate in accordance with s33 Partnership Act 1890. The deceased's share for the purposes of Confirmation will usually be a capital sum as brought down by the final accounts of the partnership.

There may however be assets vested in them such as interests in land held in the name of the deceased and previous partners as trustees for the partnership which will require to be dealt with in the Confirmation application in order to enable the asset to be sold or transferred.

Therefore make sure that you check the title to assets that form part of the business in case any action is required in the Confirmation application to transfer the title.

Share in private companies

These are shares in traditionally family-owned companies. You will need to ascertain the type and number of shares that the deceased held. While Companies House can provide some information, you will not necessarily be able to establish all of the information you will need to proceed with Confirmation. You will therefore require the assistance of the Company Secretary if there is one and the company's accountant. You will also need to acquire three years of accounts for the company (or as many sets of accounts as are available where the company is less than 3 years old). The accountant for the company should be able to establish the value per share for the deceased's shares in the company which may be more or less than other shareholder's depending on whether the deceased was either a majority or a minority shareholder in the company.

You should also check what the position is with the disposal of the shares for later on in the estate. Often private companies have limitations on who can acquire the shares, for example, a direction that the shares must be offered to other shareholders first before any transfer to an external party can be undertaken. This can be checked in the incorporation documents for the company at Companies House[41].

Shares in listed companies

A listed company is a public company whose shares are listed on a recognised stock exchange either in the UK or abroad. The most common exchanges in the UK are the London Stock Exchange (LSE) and the Alternative Investment Market (AIM).

41 https://www.gov.uk/get-information-about-a-company

While it is increasingly common for listed companies to move to non-certificated holdings in electronic format i.e. you receive a statement detailing the number and type of shares held rather than accumulating individual share certificates, it is still possible to have certificated shares in listed companies. You will need to write to the Registrar to ascertain the amount and type of shares held as at the date of death and whether share certificates will be required to sell or transfer the holding.

When trying to ascertain who the registrar for a company is, search online for the name of the company plus "investor relations". That will normally bring up the details of the registrar if there is one or will otherwise provide contact details for the company itself if their register of shareholders is maintained in house.

Once you know the type and amount of shares held in each company, you will need to undertake what is known as a quarter up valuation which will be used to obtain Confirmation and calculate the inheritance tax due. In order to calculate the quarter up value, you will need the high and low values on the date of death (where the death was at the weekend, you can use the value on either the Friday before or the Monday after the death). Historic share values can be found on sites such as https://finance.yahoo.com/quote/yhoo/history/ or https://www.hl.co.uk/help/dealing/share-dealing/share-prices2/can-i-find-historic-share-prices

The quarter up calculation is as follows:

Step 1: High value – low value = X

Step 2: low value + (X/4) = price per share on date of death

You will also need to ascertain from the registrar if there are dividends which were declared on or before the death but which had not been paid at the date of death as these will also need to be narrated on the Confirmation. These are known as ex-dividends or XD.

In addition, you should ask the registrars if there is any cash outstanding at the date of death such as uncashed dividends or dissentients funds (these are funds usually issued to shareholders where a company takeover has happened and the shareholder did not consent to the takeover but it happened regardless) as again these will need to be declared on the Confirmation application.

Where you have found share certificates, you should ask the registrar to confirm the share certificates that are valid for the holding as you will need these should you have to sell or transfer the shares. It also gives you time to try and trace any missing share certificates before the point at which you need them post Confirmation. If you do not have all of the share certificates, the Executors will need to complete an indemnity for the missing share certificates to enable a new share certificate for the balance of the missing share certificates to be issued before the affected shares can be sold or transferred. There is a cost to this which for small shareholdings can be a significant deduction against the funds actually received. It is therefore always worthwhile looking for the share certificates to avoid this scenario arising.

You will also need details of the dividends declared in the tax year to date of death and the previous tax year to calculate whether there are sums due to or by HMRC to the estate.

Foreign Shares

In addition to the requirements for UK registered shareholdings above, it will be necessary to narrate a conversion rate from the local currency on the Confirmation application eg at a rate of 0.80 Euro to £1 GB. Sites such www.xe.com will let you work out the applicable currency conversion rate at the date of death.

Share Portfolio

Where the deceased held a portfolio of shares with a stockbroker, the broker will be able to provide you with a quarter up valuation of the assets held along with details of where the asset is situated, cash outstanding and ex-dividends.

Other Investments

Valuations for other investments such as investment bonds can be obtained directly from the asset holder. If the Bond ceases on death, there may be tax consequences for the estate. See chapter 17 for further information.

National Savings & Investments

As with the assets above, you will need to ascertain the capital balance and any interest which has accrued to date of death.

Premium Bonds are a type of savings mechanism. Holders of Premium Bonds do not receive interest on their savings but receive an entry into a monthly prize draw for every £1 bond they hold. Prizes range from £25 to £1m every month. Savers can have a maximum of £50,000 invested in Premium Bonds at any one time. All prizes are free of income tax and capital gains tax. Bonds can remain in the draw for up to 1 year after the death of the deceased. On the first anniversary, the bonds plus any prizes will be repaid. Prizes won during the period of administration are also free of income tax and capital gains tax.

Life Policies

Life policy companies will usually insist on seeing the original death certificate before they will determine what the claim amount is, if any. You will need to check the letter they provide you with the details as the final claim amount may well be different from the value as at date of death due to fluctuating investment elements (if applicable), final bonuses and interest. Particularly where Inheritance Tax is an issue or legal rights are applicable, you do not wish to overstate the amount that it is due to the estate.

State Benefits

When writing to the Department for Work and Pensions, you will need to enquire about the type of benefits claimed by the deceased (including state pension), whether there are any sums due to or by the estate and obtain details of the beneficiaries paid in the current tax year to date of death and the previous tax year.

It is also helpful to contact the Recovery from Estates division of the Department of Work and Pensions where the deceased was in receipt of means tested benefits to ensure that there are no refunds due to the Department of Work and Benefits for incorrectly claimed benefits. The cross over to incorrectly claimed benefits can occur without fraud, for example, in situations such as the deceased entered long term nursing care and cancellation of benefits such as attendance allowance were not undertaken prior to the deceased's death as no one had authority to act on the recipient's behalf before they died.

Private Pensions

Depending on the nature of the pension scheme, it is likely that other than a week or two's pension falling due to the estate, the remainder of the pension will fall outwith the estate.

The payment of death benefits from most private pensions currently falls outwith the estate and will be at the discretion of the pension trustees. Not all schemes will fall out with the estate though and therefore you should check with the scheme provider before making that assumption. Where the pension falls out with the estate, this does not mean that you do not have to deal with the pension however. In most cases, you will still need to supply the death certificate, a copy of the Will and details of the close relatives of the deceased. You will also need to advise whether there was anyone financially dependent on the deceased such as a spouse or civil partner or minor children to enable the pension provider to make a decision regarding who is entitled to what from the death benefits of the pension.

While many people put in a place a nomination form or expression of wishes form to determine who should inherit the death benefits from the pension, this is by no means guaranteed and the pension trustees have the ability to settle the pension benefits with whomever they see fit.

TIP – Please note however that following the UK budget in October 2024, pensions are due to be brought back into the inheritance tax arena from 2027. It is anticipated that the pension companies will collect and pay the inheritance tax due on the pension. How that will work in practice remains to be seen, particularly for small pensions that may be under the nil rate band or for estates where the value of the pension combined with the assets in the estate are under the nil rate band. Pensions may therefore become a complicated aspect of estate administration in the future.

Membership Cards

Membership cards will let you identify groups that the deceased may have joined. Any paid for memberships will need to be cancelled and you may find that a partial refund will be due to the estate.

Loyalty schemes

It is always worth writing away to loyalty schemes as sometimes accrued points and vouchers can be transferred to a beneficiary.

Trusts and Other Estates

Where the deceased was entitled to a legacy or share of another estate or Trust, you will need to establish what is left to be transferred to the deceased and narrate the same on the Confirmation.

Where the deceased was a beneficiary of a trust, you will need to identify the type of trust and the nature of the deceased's entitlement from the trust as depending on the entitlement, this may mean that the value of the trust will need to be aggregated with the value of the estate at date of death and Inheritance Tax assessed against the total value of the combined estate and trust. This could result in the estate paying inheritance tax where it would not otherwise be payable due to the size of the estate (See Chapter Six for further information).

Credit cards

Before you write to a credit card company to advise of the death, make sure you check with the family to see whether there are any extra cards on the credit account. This is because the credit card company will cancel all cards on the account on notification of the death where it is the principal card holder that has died which may leave a spouse or child or other dependant without access to funds. This can be a particular problem where there is no joint bank account or where a joint bank account has insufficient funds to support the card holder and the sole accounts are frozen pending receipt of Confirmation.

On notification of death, the credit card company will normally freeze the account so that no further interest accrues. If there is a debit balance which is due to be paid by the estate and the credit card company is also the deceased's bank, they will usually settle the balance from the funds held in the deceased's bank account before it is closed or in part if the debt exceeds the balance held in the bank accounts.

Loans

These can usually be identified from the direct debits or standing orders details supplied by the deceased's bank. The lender will be able to confirm the sums due at the date of death and depending on the lender may freeze the interest accruing for a period of time to give the Executor time to administer the estate.

As with credit cards, where the lender is also the deceased's bank, the balance may be cleared from the deceased's bank accounts before any excess balance is paid over to the estate.

Mail order

You will need to check whether the deceased had any mail order accounts for example with Next, Very, Littlewoods etc. If there are no direct debits or standing orders showing and nothing which has come through by a mail redirection, another way to check whether the deceased had such an account is to look back over the deceased's bank statements to see if there are any card payments to such vendors.

Utilities

You will usually be able to locate the deceased's utility providers through the direct debits section of their bank account. If no direct debits can be located, you can trace their gas and electric suppliers online[42].

Council Tax

Where the deceased was the sole occupier of the property, an exemption can usually be obtained for 6 months to give the Executor time to administer the estate. Where the property hasn't been capable of being sold during that time, it will ultimately depend on the council as to whether they will continue to apply a full exemption or apply a reduced rate of council tax. Where the property is lying empty for a long time, penalty council tax may apply.

Where after the death, there is a single adult continuing to reside at the property, a single person's exemption should be applied for to reduce that person's council tax.

42 https://www.ofgem.gov.uk/information-consumers/energy-advice-households/finding-your-energy-supplier-or-network-operator

HMRC

Arrange for your Executors to complete form P1000 and submit to HMRC to have the final tax details of the deceased sent to you.[43] You can also request copies of the deceased last tax return (if applicable) which will then let you cross reference your inventory of assets against what the deceased submitted to ensure that you have not omitted any assets.

Employer

If your deceased was still in employment at the time of their death, you will need to enquire with the employer if there is any salary, holiday or sick pay due to the deceased. Your employer should also be able to advise if your deceased was entitled to any death in service benefits or pension provision.

Funeral Expenses

Frequently the funeral will have been arranged and paid for before you are instructed to act. In those circumstances, find out who has paid what for the funeral including the funeral, celebrants fees, music, orders of service, flowers and funeral tea (purvey or wake) as they will need to be refunded from the estate. You will also need these details as the funeral expenses will be a deductible expense against the assets of the estate for the purposes of calculating inheritance tax due on the estate.

Tell Us Once

The person registering the death will receive a form with codes for the Tell Us Once service. This service lets you register the death with most government departments at once and should in theory, stop or at least limit any overpayments occurring.

---

43 https://assets.publishing.service.gov.uk/media/66f540823b919067bb482776/P1000_form.pdf

Mail Redirection

You should consider whether a mail redirection should be put on the deceased's property where it is lying empty. While many asset holders and lenders are putting accounts online, particularly where your deceased has been an elderly person, they may still receive paper statements which will help you track down assets.

Lost bank account search

This is a free useful tool from the British Bankers Association[44] which enables you to check for dormant bank accounts. You complete the details online and the banks, building societies and National Savings and Investments will check their records and come back to you. While in my experience 9 times out of 10 there will be nothing to be found, my biggest hit on using this service led to me finding around £450,000 with Santander when there had been no paperwork in the house whatsoever which indicated an account with them. Likewise for another estate, I found around £250,000 in dormant accounts as a consequence of using this service. More often than not, the results that will come back will be for Premium Bonds which will quite frequently have been bought several decades ago when it was common to buy premium bonds as a gift on the birth of a child or for a 21st birthday.

Intellectual Property

Intellectual property can include trademarks, copyright and patents and is a separate right distinct from the work it relates to e.g. an author publishes a book for people to read but retains the copyright to the work so that it cannot be reproduced without permission.

As Intellectual property may subsist for many years after the date of the death, this can cause issues as depending on the age of the appointed

44 https://www.mylostaccount.org.uk/

Executor, they may not survive the requisite period to fulfil the administration of the estate!

You will also need to check that in relation to registered design rights and trademarks that deadlines for renewing do not get missed during the administration of the estate.

Digital Assets

Digital Assets are things such as bitcoin, social media accounts, domain addresses and email accounts. If the deceased did not leave a paper trail of their digital assets, it can be near impossible to identify digital assets in the estate. Particularly in the case of bitcoin, where details of how to access the asset have been left, it can mean that the asset becomes inaccessible which can mean a significant loss of value to the estate.

General

In all cases, you should always ask assets holders as part of initial investigations if there are any other products held with them, either in the sole name of the deceased or jointly with another to ensure that you have caught all assets.

CHAPTER SIX

ASSETS IN TRUST

Trust assets are normally separate entities distinct from estates. There are however certain circumstances whereby you will need to deal with trust assets as part of the estate administration process.

Assets written in Trust

Frequently, life policies and bonds are written in trust on the advice of financial advisers. The trusts used to hold the assets are frequently 'off the shelf trusts' which have been provided by the asset provider with blank spaces to be completed by hand to narrate the settlor, trustees, beneficiaries and what is being written into trust as opposed to a bespoke trust which has been drafted by a solicitor. These products will usually have had their assets written in trust and promptly forgotten about until the death occurs. You will usually find out about the trust when you write to the life insurance company and they advise that they cannot provide you with any information relating to the policy as it is written in trust.

When this happens, you need to contact the asset holder and ask for the details of the trustees as you will need certain information from the trustees in order to properly report the estate to HMRC. The asset holder will normally either provide you with the contact details or they will allow you to send a letter addressed to the trustees to them for them to pass on.

Information you need to know about a trust which was settled by the deceased is as follows:

- Who the current trustees are
- A copy of the trust deed

- Date of settlement
- The dates and amounts of settlements into the trust by the deceased as these will need to be assessed for gift reporting for Inheritance Tax purposes.

Where the deceased was the beneficiary of a trust, you will need to ascertain the following:

- The type of trust, with particular reference to whether the value of the trust, in whole or in part, requires to be aggregated with the value of the deceased's estate for the purposes of assessing inheritance tax;
- Whether there are any sums due to the deceased from the trust that had not been paid over in full prior to the death

Where the trust deed refers to instructions that can be provided by the deceased as either settlor or beneficiary by Will, you will also need to share a copy of the Will with the trustees so that they can manage the trust effectively.

Last trustee standing

Where you are advised or discover that the deceased is the last trustee of a trust, nothing can happen with the trust assets until Confirmation to the estate is obtained. Once Confirmation to the estate has been obtained, the deceased's Executors will then become the trustees[45] and be able to take steps with the trust estate, notwithstanding that the trust assets do not form part of the estate nor will not necessarily be distributed according to the terms of the deceased's Will. See chapter 7 for further information.

[45] S6 Executors (Scotland) Act 1900 as amended

When trusts can trigger Inheritance Tax in an estate

There are situations in which the death of a beneficiary of a trust can trigger a charge to Inheritance Tax in an estate. This will occur where the deceased was a beneficiary of one of the following types of trusts:

1. Bare trust;

2. Immediate post death life interest trust (IPDI);

3. Trust for a vulnerable beneficiary; or

4. Personal injury trust

A bare trust is a trust in which the assets are controlled by the trustees but which ultimately belong to one or more beneficiaries. It is a structure that is frequently used for minor beneficiaries in which the trustees control the assets until the child becomes 18 and thereafter the beneficiary can direct what happens to the trust fund.

An immediate post death life interest trust (IPDI) is one which is created on death under the terms of a Will. It grants the liferenter (who will be our deceased) the right to enjoy the income of the trust fund but they will never (usually) own the capital of the trust.

A trust for a vulnerable beneficiary is a trust with a valid vulnerable beneficiary election[46]. It can apply to trusts set up for children under 18 by their parent who has died or trusts set up for disabled persons eligible for certain state benefits[47] (although interestingly, they do not need to be

---

[46] https://www.gov.uk/government/publications/trusts-and-estates-vulnerable-person-election-form-vpe1

[47] At the time of drafting of this book, attendance allowance, disability living allowance, personal independent payment, increased disablement pension, constant attendance allowance, armed forces independence payment and child disability payment and the Scottish equivalents as and when released.

in actual receipt of the same – just meet the eligibility criteria (which begs the question that if the person was eligible surely they ought to be making a claim but that is something to ponder another time!).

A personal injury trust is a trust that is set up to hold the award compensation from a personal injury settlement. The purpose of the trust is to put the funds outwith the recipient's estate for the purposes of being assessed for means tested benefits. The settlor is the person who has been injured and must be able to obtain a benefit from the trust. As the funds in the trust had been paid out to compensate the recipient for certain losses be it limbs, ability to work etc, the trust is usually (but please check the trust deed for its terms as it is not automatic) not subject to the usual relevant property trust tax regime and has the (usually) more favourable personal tax treatment that applies to the settlor/beneficiary. Please note that a personal injury trust may also qualify as a trust for vulnerable beneficiary[48].

In all of the above situations, the value of the trust at the time of the death will be aggregated with the value of the beneficiary's estate. Where the combination of the personal estate and trust assets exceed the nil rate band, Inheritance Tax at the estate rate of 40% will be payable on the excess (less any applicable allowances and reliefs). The Inheritance Tax due is thereafter pro-rated between the trust and the estate and settled from the respective trust and estate assets before distribution to the respective beneficiaries takes place.

Example

A dies having been a liferenter of their late Aunt's Will Trust. A's net estate at date of death was worth £250,000. The Trust also has to be revalued as at the date of death of the liferenter and is revalued at

48 For further information on Personal Injury Trusts, see "A Practical Guide to Personal Injury Trusts – 2nd Edition" by Alan Robinson available from Law Brief Publishing.

£750,000. A's estate qualifies for the nil rate band only. Accordingly, inheritance tax is due across the estate and trust as follows:

A's net estate	£250,000
Aunt's Trust	£750,000
Total estate	£1,000,000
Less	
NRB	£325,000
Estate subject to IHT	£675,000
Tax due thereon @ 40%	£270,000
Tax payable by estate	(£250,000/£1m) x £270,000 = £ 67,500
Tax payable by trust	(£750,000/£1m) x £270,000 = £202,500

Gifts

Settlements into trust may require to be called back into account when calculating the Inheritance Tax due on estate.

Where a chargeable lifetime transfer (CLT) has been made into a trust which exceeds the nil rate band and the Settlor dies within 7 years of making the settlement, Inheritance Tax will fall due on the balance above the nil rate band. A CLT occurs where a gift becomes immediately chargeable to inheritance tax and usually occurs where gifts are made into a trust that are not covered by any of the inheritance tax reliefs. In these circumstances, the settlor may have paid inheritance tax at the time of settlement at the lifetime inheritance tax rate of 20% on the balance above the nil rate band. This 20% lifetime tax charge will act as a credit towards the estate rate of Inheritance Tax which falls due upon the death. However in certain cases, the 7-year window can be extended to 14 years from 7 years as part of the backwards shadow rule (see chapter 16 for further information)

CHAPTER SEVEN

APPLYING FOR CONFIRMATION

When dealing with an estate, you need to know what type of Confirmation you need to apply for on behalf of the Executors.

What is Confirmation?

Confirmation is a certificate from the Court confirming the Executors authority to intromit with the assets.

More often than not, you just need a regular Confirmation to the estate, the application for which is completed on form C1(2021)[49] for deaths on or before 31 December 2021 or form C1(2022)[50] for deaths on or after 1 January 2022. This procedure is used where no one has previously obtained Confirmation to the estate. It is also used where the persons applying for Confirmation are the Executors Nominate (testate) or Executors Dative (intestate) of the deceased or where Confirmation is being applied for by a beneficiary under S3 Executors (Scotland) Act 1900 where for whatever reason the executor appointment in a Will has failed eg all of the Executors have died, declined to act, resigned without assuming another person in their place or become incapax.

49 https://assets.publishing.service.gov.uk/media/61c08eaa8fa8f5037e8ccdc4/C1-2021.pdf

50 https://assets.publishing.service.gov.uk/media/6256d694d3bf7f60013f59e4/C1-2022.pdf

Before you begin

Before you begin drafting your application for Confirmation, you should collate the information you will need to complete the application so that it is all to hand. You will need the following information:

1. For Testate Estates, you will need the original or extract Will along with any original or extract Codicils[51], letters or deeds of declinature, deeds of resignation, deeds of assumption and/or deeds of assumption, resignation and conveyance and any Deeds of Variation executed prior to obtaining Confirmation;

2. For Intestate Estates, you will need details of the Interlocutor narrating the appointment of your Executors;

3. The details of the deceased, including name, address, date of birth, date of death, occupation and place of death. All of this information can be found on the full paid for version of the death certificate (the free abbreviated death certificate will not provide all of this information);

4. The Executors full names and current addresses;

5. Where the deceased was domiciled. This will normally be at the sheriff court in the sheriffdom local to where they lived. Where the person was of no fixed abode or where there is a foreign domiciled deceased with assets in Scotland, the relevant court will be Edinburgh Sheriff Court;

---

[51] Extract Wills and Codicils (and indeed Deeds of Assumption and/or Resignation as well as Deeds of Variation) are those which have been sent to the Books of Council and Session at Registers of Scotland for preservation. They stand in place of the original documents and can be exhibited to the Court in place of the original documents.

6. Details of the individual assets of the deceased including details of the asset holder, the address for the asset holder, customer account number or description of the asset, the share of the asset belonging to the deceased and the value of the asset;

7. The value of the funeral expenses and any debts at date of death;

8. The relatives that survived the deceased, namely spouse/civil partner, cohabiting partner, children, parents and siblings; and

9. The value of the inheritance tax due on the estate and the inheritance tax reference number allocated to the estate. It takes around 3 weeks for this code to be issued by HMRC and therefore please ensure that you leave sufficient time to obtain the code[52]. The code can be applied for online or by post.

If you are claiming either or both of the Transferable Nil Rate Band or Transferable Residential Enhancement to the Nil Rate Band, you will also need the following:

1. The Will of the first spouse/civil partner to die (if there was one);

2. A copy of the Confirmation of the first spouse/civil partner to die (if granted)[53];

---

52 https://www.gov.uk/paying-inheritance-tax/get-a-reference-number

53 Confirmations granted in or before 1999 can be obtained from the National Records of Scotland – https://www.nrscotland.gov.uk/records-and-archives/accessing-our-search-rooms/legal-search-services/. Copies of Confirmations granted in or after 2000 can be obtained from Edinburgh Sheriff Court Commissary Team – . https://www.scotcourts.gov.uk/courts-and-tribunals/courts-tribunals-and-office-locations/find-us/edinburgh-sheriff-court-and-justice-of-the-peace-court/. Fees will apply to obtain a copy of the Confirmation (and Will if applicable) for both services.

3. The value of the estate of the first spouse/civil partner to die; and

4. Whether legal rights were claimed in the estate of the first spouse/civil partner to die and details of any part of the estate that passed to someone other than the spouse as this can affect the value of the nil rate band available to transfer to your now deceased.

Where a claim will utilise two or more previous spouses/civil partners estates, you will need the same information for each predeceasing spouse/civil partner.

Completing the Application for Confirmation

Page 1 of the C1 (2021) and C1 (2022)

To complete this page, you will need to include the following information:

Your name and address – this should be the name and address of your firm. Also include your DX address (if you have one) on the bottom line.

Your reference – this is your case reference for the administration of the estate.

HM Revenue & Customs Reference – this is the reference allocated to the case by HMRC in situations where there is Inheritance Tax to pay or where there are other situations which dictate a reference is required. If there is no tax to pay and your estate is exempt from inheritance tax by operation of the deceased's nil rate band plus any transferable nil rate band, you will not have a reference and this box should be left blank.

The following boxes should be completed with the deceased's information:

1. Title

2. First Names – this is the first and middle names of the deceased. If the deceased was known by one or more names for the purposes of doing business, it is acceptable to include both eg Mary or Myra or Mary otherwise known as Myra.

3. Surname – where the deceased was known by two surnames, for example, a married woman who kept some of her assets in her maiden name and some in her married name, it is acceptable to say for example, Christie or Carmichael.

4. Address – this should be the deceased's last known permanent address which could be a care home rather than either an owned or rented residential property.

5. Occupation – where the deceased was retired, this should be included in the narration eg Retail Worker (retired), Doctor (retired) etc

6. Date of Birth

7. Date of death

8. Place of Death – this will be narrated on the full version of the death certificate. It is not always possible to include the full place of death in the Confirmation. It is therefore acceptable to say At Home or an abbreviated format such as Wishaw General Hospital. Where possible, I put the first line of the place or address plus the postcode.

9. Total Estate for Confirmation – this is the gross value of assets being confirmed too within the jurisdictions of Great Britain and Northern Ireland. It does not include assets abroad or assets held in trust where the deceased was a trustee rather than a beneficiary.

10. Full name and address of each Executor – the executors should be listed in the same order as they narrated in the Will then any

Codicils and thereafter any executors who have been assumed by existing Executors. Include their full name and current address.

<u>Page 2 of the C1 (2021) and C1 (2022)</u>

The following should be completed:

Declaration by – this should be the first named Executor where possible. You need to include their full name and address eg John Smith residing at The Smithy, Bloggsville, KY16 7PY. The name and address of the Executor should match the details provided on page 1 of the application.

Who declares that the deceased – insert full name of the deceased per the front page.

Domiciled in – this should narrate both the sheriffdom and court in which the deceased was domiciled in eg the Sherifdom of Glasgow and Strathkelvin at Glasgow in Scotland or the Sheriffdom of North Strathclyde at Paisley in Scotland.

That I am – As part of the Confirmation process, you will need to draft a declaration on page 2 of the application for execution by the Executors which will include the following information

1. How the Executors are acting eg by nominate, dative or S3 Executors (Scotland) Act 1900 appointment;

2. Where it is a testate estate, narrates any discrepancies within the Will to the present circumstances eg change of surname or address of the testator or Executor or the death or retirement of an Executor;

3. Refers to the documents being supplied with the application and whether they are original documents, certified copies or registered extracts and that they have been docketed and signed as relative to the application;

The declaration is effectively a story about the deceased, the relevant documents relating to the management of their affairs on their death and how the Executors named on page 1 of the application for Confirmation have title to act.

Example 1

Bryan Jones died intestate on 13 October 2024. His daughter, Mrs Stella Plimco residing at 123 Joe Bloggs Road, Bloggsville, KY13 4PY was appointed as his Executrix Dative Qua Daughter of the Full Blood by interlocutor dated 4 March 2024 at Edinburgh Sheriff Court.

The declaration in these circumstances may read as:

Executrix Dative qua daughter of the full blood conform to Interlocutor granted by Sheriff ABC at Edinburgh Sheriff Court in the Sheriffdom of Lothian and Borders on 4 March 2024.

Example 2

Mrs April Jones dies on 1 January 2024 having her home address at 123 Joe Bloggs Road, Bloggsville, KY13 4PY. Her Will was validly executed on 19 February 2015. At the time of writing the Will, Mrs Jones resided at Valhalla, Priory Bridge Road, Bloggsville, KY13 4YZ. None of the details regarding the appointment of her Executor had changed. The original Will is being exhibited for Confirmation.

The declaration in these circumstances may read as:

Executor Nominate conform to the Will of the deceased dated 19 February 2015. In said Will, the deceased is designed as residing at Valhalla, Priory Bridge Road, Bloggsville, KY13 4YZ. The original Will is docquetted, signed and exhibited as relative hereto.

Example 3

Per the Example above, but this time, Mrs Jones has appointed two Executors to act – Mr Paul Jones also residing at 123 Joe Bloggs Road, Bloggsville, KY13 4PY and Miss Christine McCance residing at 45 Hillhead Road, Bloggsville, KY12 4RC. Christine predeceased Mrs Jones on 14 December 2023.

The declaration in these circumstances may read as:

Executor Nominate conform to the Will of the deceased dated 19 February 2015. In said Will, the deceased is designed as residing at Valhalla, Priory Bridge Road, Bloggsville, KY13 4YZ. In said Will, Miss Christine McCance residing at 45 Hillhead Road, Bloggsville, KY12 4RC is designed as Executor. The said Miss Christine McCance predeceased the deceased on 14 December 2023. The original Will is docquetted, signed and exhibited as relative hereto.

Example 4

Mrs April Jones dies on 1 January 2024 having her home address at 123 Joe Bloggs Road, Bloggsville, KY13 4PY. Her Will was validly executed on 19 February 2015. At the time of writing the Will, Mrs Jones resided at Valhalla, Priory Bridge Road, Bloggsville, KY13 4YZ. Mrs Jones appointed two Executors to act per her Will – Mr Paul Jones also residing at 123 Joe Bloggs Road, Bloggsville, KY13 4PY and Miss Christine McCance residing at 45 Hillhead Road, Bloggsville, KY12 4RC. At the time of Mrs Jones's death, Miss Christine McCance was residing at The Strand, 321 London Road, London SW1 2PQ. Mrs Jones had also executed a Codicil leaving £5,000 to her favourite charity dated 16 June 2023. Both the Will and Codicil were registered in the Books of Council and Session on 4 February 2024.

The declaration in these circumstances may read as:

Executor Nominate conform to the Will of the deceased dated 19 February 2015 and Codicil dated 16 June 2023, both of which were registered in the Books of Council and Session on 4 February 2024 along with Miss Christine McCance residing at The Strand, 321 London Road, London SW1 2PQ. In said Will and Codicil, the deceased is designed as residing at Valhalla, Priory Bridge Road, Bloggsville, KY13 4YZ. In said Will, Miss Christine McCance is designed as residing at 45 Hillhead Road, Bloggsville, KY12 4RC. An extract of the Will and Codicil are docquetted, signed and exhibited as relative hereto.

Example 5

The circumstances are the same per Example 4 except Christine McCance and Paul Jones assumed Paula Paton of 3 Queensland Court, Bloggsville, KY10 7RN as an Executor and Paul Jones resigned as an Executor by a Deed dated 12 and 14 January 2024 which was also registered in the Books of Council and Session on 13 February 2024.

The declaration in these circumstances may read as:

Executor Nominate conform to the Will of the deceased dated 19 February 2015 and Codicil dated 16 June 2023, both of which were registered in the Books of Council and Session on 4 February 2024 and Deed of Assumption, Resignation and Conveyance dated 12 and 14 January 2024 and registered in the Books of Council and Session on 13 February 2024 along with Paula Paton residing at 3 Queensland Court, Bloggsville, KY10 7RN. In said Will and Codicil, the deceased is designed as residing at Valhalla, Priory Bridge Road, Bloggsville, KY13 4YZ. In said Will, Miss Christine McCance is designed as residing at 45 Hillhead Road, Bloggsville, KY12 4RC. An extract of the Will, Codicil and Deed of Assumption, Resignation and Conveyance are docquetted, signed and exhibited as relative hereto.

> **TIP** – Where you have a lengthy declaration for example because all Executors and the testators have moved address or changed surname, there are multiple documents which require to be narrated and referred to or you have a corporate Executor that has a lengthy narration about how the person signing on behalf of the organisation can act and it will not fit in the declaration box, you can type up the declaration in Word and label it "Declaration to the inventory of the estate of the late (insert name of deceased) – Paper Apart" and have the Executor sign underneath the declaration. This is then slotted into the Confirmation application between pages 2 and 3. In the declaration section on section 2 on page 2 of the C1 you insert the words "please see paper apart".

That I – insert full name of Executor signing the form

along with .... – insert the full names of all other Executors in whose names Confirmation should be granted. This should mirror the order detailed on Page 1 of the Application. If there is a sole executor, once the application is printed, put a line through all wording starting with "along with" and ask the Executor to initial at the side.

That I do not know of any testamentary settlement or writing relating to the disposal of the deceased's estate or any part of the deceased's estate other than that mentioned in paragraph 2 – while nothing needs to be completed at this paragraph, it is important to ensure that both you and the Executor read the wording here. In circumstances where the Will has went missing or otherwise is not formally valid but the terms of the Will mirror the distribution that would happen on intestacy, it may be entirely practical to treat the estate as an intestate one for the purposes of obtaining Confirmation rather than going to the delay and expense that would occur were you to arrange to set up a copy Will to be admitted to the Confirmation process. This paragraph however requires the executor to declare that they do not know of any testamentary writing other than that (if any) referred to in their declaration at section 2 on page 2. It is therefore in direct conflict with this declaration for the estate to be dealt with on intestacy where a Will exists.

That the inventory (on pages 3 to __) is a full and complete inventory of ...... – Once the application has been printed off, you will need to write the page number in the box. For reasons best known to HMRC, they do not let you type in this box before printing. I normally use page numbers in the format 3a, 3b, 3c etc if for no other reason than the page in the Confirmation after page 3 is page 4 and therefore continuing the numerical numbering just doesn't work. 3i, 3ii etc would also work as would capital letters or capital Roman numerals.

That confirmation of the estate in Scotland, England and Wales and Northern Ireland amounting in value to ________________ is required – Insert the same figure as you have on Page 1 which should match the total on the Summary for Confirmation on page 3 plus any additional inventory pages that you have included.

To the best of my knowledge and belief the information I have given in this form is correct and complete – this section needs to be signed and dated by your first named executor. Your Executor should also sign and date any documents being presented to the court on the same day as signing the application for Confirmation. Only the lead Executor requires to sign the Confirmation application but if the estate requires to submit an IHT400, all Executors must sign that form.

Every document that is mentioned in your declaration above needs to be submitted to the Court with the application for Confirmation. Each document requires to have a docket attached to it before signing. This should be appended in the margin of the first page (not the cover) of each document in the following format:

______________ (Place of Signing) ____________ (Date of signing)

This is the [original/extract] [Will/Codicil/Letter of Declinature/Deed of Assumption, Resignation & Conveyance/Deed of Variation etc] referred to in my declaration of even date herewith to the inventory of the estate of the late John Smith

______________________________ (signed)

In terms of where in the margin the docket should go, I usually pick the margin on the document with the most space so this means sometimes it sits at the top of the page, the bottom of the page or down the side. If you are supplying multiple documents, the docket does not need to be in the same place on every document.

TIP – when preparing Wills and other documents post death that will be exhibited as part of the Confirmation process, make sure you leave a decent margin so that a docket can be appended. There is nothing worse than trying to cram a docket onto a document with next to no margin in handwriting that requires a magnifying glass to read!

The word "original" in the docket should be substituted for "extract" or "certified copy" depending on the version of the document that you have in front of you to submit.

Page 3 – Inventory

This section details all of the assets in the estate. While you are provided with one page to complete the inventory, this may not be sufficient depending on the extent of the assets your deceased has. You can either use continuation sheets (form C2[54]) or it is acceptable to type up the inventory as a paper apart. The paper apart should follow the same format and section headings as page 3 of the inventory. It should also be headed up "Inventory to the estate of the late (insert name of deceased) – Paper Apart". The paper apart should be slotted into the C1 between pages 3–4. If using a paper apart, on page 3 insert "please see paper apart" and the total being confirmed too.

I normally use Excel to prepare the paper apart – this has a threefold benefit as follows:

[54] https://assets.publishing.service.gov.uk/media/5a74a45bed915d0e8e399d75/c2_2_lined.pdf

1. If you make a mistake (we are human after all!) or an additional asset is located prior to applying for Confirmation, it is easy to amend. For reasons best known to HMRC, the forms as provided do not lend themselves well to being amended;

2. It allows you to automate cross checking of totals; and

3. It can then be saved as a new version to act as the starting point for your accounts (more of which later)

The Inventory needs to be laid out in a particular order as follows:

1. Heritable estate in Scotland

2. Moveable estate in Scotland

3. Estate in England & Wales

4. Estate in Northern Ireland

Each section needs to contain the heading, then list the relevant assets within the category and the value of each then conclude with a sub total of the category.

For each asset, you will need to detail

1. the asset holder;

2. the address of the asset holder;

3. the account/customer reference number of each asset held with the asset holder;

4. if the asset is held in joint names with one or more other owners, the share attributable to the deceased;

5. where the asset needs to be valued, for example, where it is a house, contents, jewellery, a vehicle or other mode of transport, how it was valued eg as valued for the Executors by XYZ Surveyors;

6. the value of the asset attributable to the deceased.

For land and buildings, you need to ensure you include in the description of the asset the full conveyancing description. For Land Registered titles within the UK, this is simply the appropriate title number or numbers. Be sure to include any title numbers that refer to commonly used parts that are shared with other people, for example, parking spaces. For land that remains registered in the Register of Sasines or the English or Northern Irish versions of the Register, you will need to include the full conveyancing description contained in the relevant disposition.

Each asset also needs to be listed sequentially with a number attached to it eg if you have 10 asset holders, you should have the assets listed 1-10. Similarly, if you have multiple assets with the one asset holder, individual assets with the same asset holder should be sub-labelled a, b, c or I, ii, iii etc

Example

Heritable Estate in Scotland

1. 123 Acacia Avenue, Bloggsville, KY12 4TY

   All as more properly described in Land Certificate

   Title Sheet no BLO123456

   As valued for the Executors by XYZ Surveyors £340,000

   Total heritable estate in Scotland £340,000

Example

Moveable Estate In Scotland

2. Personal Effects

   Contents of 123 Acacia Avenue, aforesaid

   As valued for the Executors by ABC Auction House £ 1,250

3. TSB PLC

   52-60 St Vincent Street, Glasgow, G2 5TU

   Direct Saver Account No: 654321/12345678

   Balance at date of death £200,000

   Interest accrued to death but not yet paid £ 1,000

   Total moveable estate in Scotland **£202,250**

Example

Estate in England and Wales

4. National Savings & Investments

   Sunderland, SR43 2SB

   a. Direct Saver Account No: 321654/56781234

      Balance at date of death £200,000

      Interest accrued to death but not yet paid £ 1,000

   b. Premium Bonds

Holder No: 123123123123

Balance at date of death £ 50,000

Prizes accrued to death but not yet paid £ 100

Total estate in England & Wales **£251,100**

Example

Estate in England and Wales

5. National Savings & Investments

Sunderland, SR43 2SB

a. Direct Saver Account No: 654321/12345678

Held jointly with spouse

Balance at date of death £200,000

Whereof one half share £100,000

Interest accrued to death but not yet paid £ 1,000

Whereof one half share £ 500

b. Premium Bonds

Holder's number: 12312323

Balance at date of death £ 50,000

Prizes accrued to death but not yet paid £ 100

Total estate in England & Wales **£150,600**

Chapter 10 of Currie on Confirmation provides excellent references for narrating various assets in the application for Confirmation.

Once you have narrated all of the assets on the inventory, you need to provide a summary for Confirmation at the end of the asset list which should take the following format:

Summary for Confirmation

Heritable Estate in Scotland	£230,000
Moveable Estate in Scotland	£ 15,345
Estate in England & Wales	£ 50,000
Estate in Northern Ireland	Nil
Total Estate for Confirmation	£295,345

The total for Confirmation should match the total on pages 1 and 2 of the application for Confirmation and also on page 4.

I also usually add at the bottom of each page of the paper apart, page 3a, page 3b etc and where asked for the number of pages of the inventory on page 2, add the last page number eg 3d. This can either be added manually with pen once the inventory has been printed or you can add it to the bottom of your inventory on excel, word etc – just make sure that if you are moving assets around that the page numbers land in the correct places and you don't find them in the middle of your document!

Page 4

For the summary at the top of the form, carry forward the total assets for Confirmation from the inventory at page 3. Thereafter complete each of the boxes at 12 -14 with the relevant amounts. If there is no debt/funeral expense, in the relevant category, complete zero in the box. Box 15 should automatically calculate the net estate however, double check this manually as sometimes the form glitches and leaves it as nil. If you cannot get it to show the total, then you may have to complete a new form to get it to work – this doesn't mean redoing the whole form, just page 4. If that still doesn't work, print off the application, put a line through the zero and manually insert the correct total. Your Executor should initial next to the amendment.

If you have completed form IHT400, tick Yes at box 16 and leave the rest of the questions on this page blank.

If you have not completed form IHT400, tick No at box 16 and then answer the rest of the questions. If for any reason, you cannot locate the national insurance of the deceased (and in most cases, you should be able to locate this from a letter from HMRC, a letter from the Department of Work and Pensions or on P60s from pensions and employment), write "not known" as some sheriff courts will reject the application if this section is not completed with either this phrase or the NI number.

Page 5

This is where the forms for deaths before and after 31 December 2021 diverge.

C1(2022)

Box 21 – tick yes or no is the estate is an excepted estate.

An Excepted Estate is one in which no inheritance tax is due because the deceased died domiciled in the UK on or after 6 April 2024, the gross value of any foreign assets included in the estate does not exceed £100,000, the gross value of any specified transfers does not exceed £250,000, the value of any trust assets included in the estate does not exceed £1m from a single trust with the net chargeable estate attributable to the trust after deduction of the spousal/civil partner allowance not exceeding £250,000 **and** one of the following conditions apply:

1. For deaths on or before 31 December 2021, the gross estate is under £1m and after deduction of spousal/civil partner relief and/or charitable relief and allowed liabilities, the net estate is less then the nil rate band; or

2. For deaths on or after 1 January 2022, the gross estate is under £3m and after deduction of spousal/civil partner relief and/or charitable relief and allowed liabilities, the net estate is less than the nil rate band.

A key point to note here is the operation of legal rights. If legal rights have not been claimed or discharged prior to applying for Confirmation, the legal rights must be deducted from the spousal exemption. If the value of the legal rights exceeds the nil rate band, it cannot be an excepted estate at the point of applying for Confirmation and Inheritance Tax will need to be paid. If the legal rights are subsequently discharged, it is thereafter possible to reclaim overpaid inheritance tax which has been paid as a consequence of the existence of the legal rights. Given legal rights claimants have up to 20 years to claim or discharge their legal rights, this should act as a particular catalyst to try and get decisions made sooner rather than later where cashflow within the estate for the purposes of paying inheritance tax may be an issue.

Box 22 – tick yes if you are claiming some or all of the nil rate band of a predeceasing spouse.

Box 23 – the gross value may, more often than not, be the same total of the estate as you have put on pages 1-4. However, it may be higher as it will also include:

1. assets which have passed outwith the estate automatically by dint of survivorship destinations eg shares of land and buildings;

2. assets held in trust which require to be accumulated with the deceased's estate for inheritance tax purposes eg immediate post death interest trusts where the deceased was the life renter or

where an election was made for the deceased to be a vulnerable beneficiary within a trust and therefore the trust was taxed during the deceased's lifetime at their personal tax rate rather than the trust tax rate;

3. Gifts made within the 7 years preceding the deceased's death;

4. The value of any gifts made by the deceased in which the deceased or their spouse/civil partner retained an interest (gift with reservation of benefit).

Box 24 – the net value of the estate should be the same total as Box 15 on page 4

Box 25 – the net qualifying value of the estate should be the net value of the estate less any spouse/civil partner and/or charity relief only. No other reliefs such as Business Property Relief or Agricultural Property Relief should be included here.

C1(2021)

Box 21 – See commentary at box 23 on C1 (2022) above.

Box 22 – See commentary at Box 24 on C1 (2022) above.

Box 23 – See commentary at Box 25 on C1 (2022) above.

Box 24 – following completion of this section you should have one "yes" and three "no" boxes checked.

An Exempt Estate is one in which inheritance tax does not apply as the estate is under the nil rate band before any reliefs apply.

An Exempt and Excepted Estate is one in which no inheritance tax is due as the estate is under the nil rate band and the excepted estate rules (see above) also apply to the estate.

If the estate does not qualify as an Exempt or an Excepted Estate you will need to complete form IHT400.

Box 25 – complete the amount of inheritance tax paid which may be nil. Please note that this figure should match the amount on the clearance letter from HMRC otherwise you run the risk that the application will be rejected by the court.

If you are claiming the transferable nil rate band, you will also need to complete form IHT402 with the details of the predeceasing spouse's estate. If you are claiming shares of more than one predeceasing spouse/civil partner's nil rate band, complete a form for each estate being claimed. You would be well advised to start collecting the information relating to the former spouse's estate as early as possible into the administration of the estate as it may take some time to locate all of the relevant information as you will need details of among other things where the couple were married, date of death of first spouse, the division of the estate and whether Confirmation was granted along with a copy of the Will, any Codicils and a copy of the Grant of Confirmation.

Assets that need to be dealt with in the Confirmation application but do not form part of the Inventory of the Estate

There are certain assets which require to be dealt with as part of the Confirmation application but which do not form part of the inventory to the estate. This can be because the assets are situated outwith the UK or for whatever reason are vested in the deceased's name as trustee. These are dealt with on the inventory but after the summary for Confirmation.

Assets held in Trust where deceased is the sole trustee

As the trust estate is not an asset of the estate and does not belong to the deceased as a personal asset, it cannot be confirmed to the usual manner. It needs to be listed after the summary of the estate has been narrated in the C1/C2.

Example

Summary for Confirmation

Heritable Estate in Scotland	£300,000
Moveable Estate in Scotland	£ 1,000
Estate in England & Wales	£ 63,000
Estate in Northern Ireland	Nil
Total Estate for Confirmation	£364,000

Assets Held in Trust

Property held in (insert name of trust) settled by a trust deed dated (insert date) by (insert name of Settlor) under the terms of which trust deed, the following property is vested in the deceased as the sole surviving and accepting trustee:

(a) Legal and General PLC

(insert address of asset holder)

Policy No: XY123456

Balance at date of death £100,000.00

(b) Cater Allen Private Bank

(insert address of asset holder)

Account number: 00000001

Balance at date of death £ 12,123.45

Once Confirmation has been granted, Confirmation will act as the link in title for the Executors to be able to:

1. Where the trust requires to continue, assign the trust property to such persons who are entitled to continue to administer the trust ie new trustees;

2. Transfer the property to entitled beneficiaries eg where the trust deed is specific in the final destination of the asset; or

3. Transfer the property to any person appointed by the beneficiaries to ingather and distribute the trust.

<u>Assets held in Partnership</u>

Likewise, where partnership property is vested in the deceased as the last surviving partner, you may use a declaration like this to link the title:

<u>Partnership Property</u>

The following property is vested in the deceased as the sole surviving and accepting trustee of the partnership known as the firm of XYZ:

1. The subjects known as Bloggsville Farm

   All as more properly described in Land Register

   Title No: BLO123456

   As valued by ABC surveyors £600,000

Foreign Assets

These assets need to be listed under the heading "Estate in Rest of World" then listed by jurisdiction and then described in the usual manner.

Example

Estate in Rest of World

Isle of Man

Canada Life International

Canada Life House, Isle of Business Park, Douglas, Isle Of Man IM2 2QJ

Bond No: 123456

Balance at date of death £60,000

United States of America

Liberty Global PLC

Computershare Investor Services, PO Box 43078, Providence,

RI 02940-3078

327 C Shares @ US$27.54 each

Converted at a rate of US£2.37 to GB £1 £3,799.82

Inheritance Tax Return

Depending on the value/composition of the assets in the estate and when your deceased died, you may also need to submit a tax return narrating the amount of inheritance tax that requires to be paid on the estate (including estates which are nil).

You need a form C5(2006)[55] where the death occurred on or prior to 31 December 2021 and there is either no inheritance tax to pay or none of the triggering events to complete an IHT400 have occurred. For death on or after 1 January 2022, no C5(2006) is required where there is no inheritance tax to pay and none of the triggering events to complete an IHT400 have occurred

An IHT400 and supplementary forms will be required where there is inheritance tax to pay or in circumstances where there is no inheritance tax to pay, but a trigger event has happened which requires an IHT400 to be completed.

You will need all of the information concerning the assets from the C1 to complete either the C5(2006) or IHT400.

Form C5 (2006)

The C5 is a short 3-page form which has two pages of questions to be answered concerning the deceased's assets and lifetime gifting. Notwithstanding there is no tax to pay, the answers to these questions may trigger the need to stop drafting the C5 and switch to completion of the IHT400. The C5 is submitted to the Sheriff Court along with your application for Confirmation.

Form IHT400

The IHT400 is a significantly lengthier form at 16 pages than the C5. The IHT400 is the summary of the asset and the Tax position. In addition to the IHT400, you will need to complete a number of supplementary forms as directed by the IHT400. The supplemental forms provide additional information for HMRC on the nature of the asset and any reliefs being claimed. The number and type of supplementary pages required will ultimately depend on the assets or

55 https://www.gov.uk/government/publications/inheritance-tax-return-of-estate-information-c5-2006

gifting made by the deceased so you are unlikely to ever have two estates that need the exact same set of supplementary forms completed.

The available supplemental forms are as follows:

1. IHT401 – Domicile outside the UK
2. IHT402 – Transferable nil rate band claim form
3. IHT403 – Gifts and other transfers of value
4. IHT404 – Jointly owned assets
5. IHT405 – Houses, land and buildings
6. IHT406 – Bank and building society accounts
7. IHT407 – Household and personal effects
8. IHT408 – Household and personal effects donated to charity
9. IHT409 – Pensions
10. IHT410 – Life assurance and annuities
11. IHT411 – Listed stocks and shares
12. IHT412 – Unlisted stocks and shares
13. IHT413 – Business and partnership assets
14. IHT414 – Agricultural relief
15. IHT415 – Interest in another estate
16. IHT416 – Debts due to the estate
17. IHT417 – Foreign assets

18. IHT418 – Assets held in trust

19. IHT419 – Debts owned by the deceased

20. IHT420 – National heritage, conditional exemption and maintenance

21. IHT421 – Probate summary

22. IHT422 – Application for an Inheritance Tax reference number

23. IHT423 – Direct payment scheme form

24. IHT430 – Reduced rate of Inheritance Tax claim form

25. IHT435 – Residence nil rate band claim form

26. IHT436 – Transferable residence nil rate band claim form

The supplemental forms that need to be completed will be different for every estate and will be dictated by the nature of the assets that are contained within your estate and the reliefs being claimed.

You can also use papers apart to the supplemental forms to provide the information requested, for example, where you have too many of the asset to fit into the boxes provided. In that case, simply write in the box "see paper apart". You may need to add the total of your figures from your paper apart onto the form to make the form work to carry through the numbers. You can also provide formal valuations such as Probate stocks and shares valuations as part of the supplemental information or you may wish to provide the relevant information in a paper apart prepared in Word or Excel or equivalent software.

> TIP – The IHT400 will round the numbers input. Cross check your inventory against the final numbers in the form to make sure nothing has been omitted. They should come to within a £1 or two of each other on rounding.

The IHT400 provides a more in-depth guide to the assets which enables HMRC to ascertain if the correct amount of Inheritance Tax has been paid. If it looks like your estate will be subject to Inheritance Tax, I would recommend that you look at the IHT400 and required supplementary forms early on in the administration of the estate as you may not receive all of the necessary information you need to complete the forms as part of the usual initial investigation response letters from asset holders.

I would recommend that you leave yourself a good couple of hours of peace and quiet to complete the Confirmation application and the IHT400 and supplementary forms so that you do not miss anything or double count an asset. There is an excellent manual that has been prepared by HMRC to assist with completing the forms[56].

HMRC will ask for copies of Wills, Confirmation applications and Powers of Attorney to be submitted with the IHT400. Do not submit the original documents as these will not be returned to you once HMRC's purposes are served.

---

[56] For deaths on or after 1 January 2022 use https://assets.publishing.service.gov.uk/government/uploads/system/uploads/attachment_data/file/1118154/IHT400-Notes-English-2022.pdf. For deaths on or before 31 December 2021, use https://assets.publishing.service.gov.uk/government/uploads/system/uploads/attachment_data/file/1046019/IHT4002021-Notes-11-21-online.pdf. Be careful to select the correct manual as there are differences depending on when the person died.

TIP – if you are tasked with the preparation or revision of initial investigation template letters for your firm, it would be worthwhile taking some time to go through each of the IHT400 and supplemental forms to find out what information may be needed from each type of asset holder to be able to complete the forms. Thereafter, you can incorporate requests into your template letters for the information needed thus streamlining the information gathering exercise.

Unlike the application for Confirmation, the IHT400 requires to be signed by all Executors.

The deadline for submission of the IHT400 is one year from date of death. Submission after this date will incur penalties even if there is no tax to pay.

Other types of Confirmation

Where Confirmation has been granted, it may be necessary to return to the Court to obtain further title to assets. This can be done in a variety of ways:

Eik – this is used in situations whereby an asset has been described incorrectly eg the number in the land certificate in the description has been transposed, or additional assets have been found that need to be confirmed too or it is found that an asset previously included in the Confirmation application have been incorrectly valued and a substitute value is required. This is applied for using Form C4(S)(2022)[57] for deaths on or after 1 January 2022 or Form C4(S)(2021)[58] for deaths on or before 31 December 2021.

57 https://assets.publishing.service.gov.uk/media/6687e171d9d351878 68f451b/C4S-2022.pdf

58 https://assets.publishing.service.gov.uk/media/6687e171899a6f92e5d9cd83/C4S-2021.pdf

The major practical problem with this form is that you cannot type on page 3. Page 3 requires narration of details from the previous Confirmation application (and any previous Eiks) as well as the person currently making the declaration. You therefore have two options:

1. Print off the page and complete it manually in pen or if your office still has one, by typewriter; or

2. Replicate the page in Word (including formatting) and complete the details and substitute your page for the page 3 in the application. The benefit of this option is that if you make a mistake, you can easily amend the form. Likewise, if there is a lot of information that you need to add to the form, it will present nicely spaced out rather than presenting as squashed up writing which will become a public record.

Unlike the application for Confirmation, an Eik requires to be signed by the lead executor twice, once on page 3 and once on page 4 and by all other Executors on page 4.

If additional tax becomes payable, do not send the original form to HMRC. Send a copy of the Eik to HMRC and confirm that you have retained the original to submit to the court. This is because HMRC will not return any documents submitted to them. Pay the inheritance tax (and interest due if any) and HMRC will arrange for a letter with the clearance code to be sent to you which you then submit with the Eik to the relevant Court.

<u>Confirmation ad omissa</u> – this is used in situations where all of the original Executors who obtained Confirmation have died, resigned or otherwise incapable of proceeding to obtain an Eik. This procedure is invoked where additional estate has been found and needs to be dealt with.

<u>Confirmation ad omissa vel male apprentia</u> – this is used in situations where all of the original Executors who obtained Confirmation have died,

resigned or otherwise incapable of proceeding to obtain an Eik and there is an asset which has been identified as having been confirmed to at under value.

Confirmation ad non executa – this is used in situations where all of the original Executors who obtained Confirmation have died, resigned or otherwise incapable of proceeding to obtain an Eik and there remains unadministered estate within the original deceased's estate which needs to be dealt with.

It is possible for an application for Confirmation ad non executa and Confirmation ad omissa to be made in a single application in circumstances where the original Executors have died, resigned or are otherwise incapable and an additional asset has been located.

Form X-1[59] is used for ad non executa and ad omissa applications.

What to ask for when applying for Confirmation

You will receive a single Confirmation booklet when you apply for Confirmation. If you only require Confirmation for a single asset, this may be sufficient for your purposes. If however you have multiple assets that you need to either sell or transfer, you will need to ask when submitting the application for Confirmation for a Certificate of Confirmation for each asset that you require to deal with otherwise you will need to wait until the Confirmation is returned from one asset holder to send to the next and so on.

If you are dealing with foreign assets, you should ask for a certified extract Confirmation (with Will annexed if required). This will be certified by a

59 https://www.scotcourts.gov.uk/rules-and-practice/forms/sheriff-court-forms/dealing-with-a-deceaseds-estate/ The link is near the bottom of the page.

Sheriff and can be sent to the Foreign and Commonwealth Office to have an Apostille appended[60] before sending abroad.

60 https://www.gov.uk/get-document-legalised

CHAPTER EIGHT

PAYMENT OF INHERITANCE TAX

When is Inheritance Tax due?

Where there is Inheritance Tax to pay, this will need to be paid before Confirmation can be granted. Inheritance Tax requires to be paid in full prior to Confirmation on all assets except land and property.

Where there is land or buildings involved, only 1/10th of the tax due on the assets needs to be paid prior to Confirmation being granted. This is because the government recognises that extracting value from properties is not easily realisable. The remainder can be paid in a further 9 x annual instalments. However, where possible, you should arrange for the Inheritance Tax due on land and buildings to be paid off as soon as possible as interest will accrue on the unpaid tax due. If the property is sold or transferred, any outstanding balance of Inheritance Tax plus interest must be paid immediately.

The deadline for paying Inheritance Tax is 6 months from the date of death. Thereafter, interest will accrue on unpaid tax.

Inheritance Tax Reference number

You will need to obtain an Inheritance Tax reference before you can pay any tax. This is done online at www.gov.uk/paying-inhertiance-tax/get-a-reference-number/. It will take around 3 weeks from application to receive the reference number so make sure you leave plenty of time to undertake this process before you need to apply for Confirmation.

Funding Inheritance Tax

The need to pay Inheritance Tax up front can lead to a bit of a chicken and egg situation. In order to gain access to the assets, you need a Grant of Confirmation. In order to get the Grant of Confirmation, you need to pay Inheritance Tax. If there are insufficient available assets that can be used to fund the Inheritance Tax due, the Executors will need to obtain a loan to meet the tax bill. This can either be on a commercial basis from a high street or specialist lender or alternatively, where one or more beneficiaries have access to funds, they can lend the estate the funds to meet the tax bill. This will then be repaid once the estate is in funds post Confirmation before any payment are made to beneficiaries of the estate in terms of the Will or per intestate succession law.

In the event that the Executors cannot raise the money to pay the Inheritance Tax due before Confirmation can be granted, they can apply for a Grant on Credit from HMRC. This will enable HMRC to postpone the payment of tax until after Confirmation has been granted and the Executors can access assets to pay the Tax. This should be a last resort as HMRC will expect your Executor to have exhausted all possible avenues of funding the Inheritance Tax before granting credit[61].

The IHT400 and supplementary forms along with a copy of the Will and Confirmation document will need to be sent to HMRC and payment of the tax made before the Court will grant Confirmation. It used to be the case that HMRC would stamp the C1 and return it to you however this has now been replaced with a letter confirming that the tax has been paid. This process can take 5-8 weeks depending on how busy HMRC are at the time of receipt of the application and therefore you need to build in sufficient time for this process to conclude before you need Confirmation. The letter from HMRC needs to be submitted to the

61 See https://www.gov.uk/hmrc-internal-manuals/inheritance-tax-manual/ihtm05122 for further information

Court with the C1 and Will (if applicable) and other relevant documents being submitted with the application.

Direct Payments Scheme

Most banks will take part in the direct payments scheme which will enable a release of funds from the deceased's bank account direct to HM Revenues and Customs. Depending on the bank, they will either send the funds by direct transfer to HMRC or they will send you a cheque made payable to HMRC for you to send on. In order to take advantage of this facility, you will need to complete form IHT423[62] for each asset holder that you wish to draw down funds from and all Executors will require to sign the forms. The asset holder may also wish to see Form IHT400 to confirm that the estate is indeed subject to Inheritance Tax.

A word of caution – while most asset holders will pay the tax directly to HMRC on receipt of the IHT423 by bank transfer, some will issue a cheque made payable to HMRC to you instead. You in turn will need to forward to HMRC. This will add anything from a couple of days to a couple of weeks into the time frame for which HMRC are credited with the tax and can therefore delay the issuing of the code letter.

Brokers

It may also be possible where the deceased held a portfolio of shares for the broker to release funds directly to HM Revenues and Customs. This usually involves the Executors having to provide an undertaking and indemnity to the broker in case it transpires that the named Executors are found not to have title to obtain Confirmation eg a closer family relative is located in the case of a dative petition or a later Will is found naming alternative Executors.

62 https://www.gov.uk/government/publications/inheritance-tax-direct-payment-scheme-bank-or-building-society-account-iht423

CHAPTER NINE

INGATHERING ASSETS

Once Confirmation has been granted, you can ingather the assets ready for distribution. This can either be done by transferring the assets directly to the relevant beneficiaries or by encashing the assets.

In order to ingather the assets, you will normally need to exhibit the Certificate of Confirmation along with a completed claim/account closure form or other legal conveyance before you can do so. Most asset holders have relatively high thresholds before insisting on sight of Confirmation which can be £10,000, £20,000 or in some cases as high as £50,000 or beyond. This means that you may well be able to get access to funds ahead of Confirmation being granted or depending on the value and type of assets held, without the need for Confirmation at all.

Property and land

Property and land can be transferred in one of two ways namely by disposition or docket transfer. A transfer by disposition will transfer the title on the Land Register. If the title was originally registered in the Sasines Register, a disposition will trigger a first registration in the Land Register. While more costly, it does mean that the recipient will have an infeft publicly recognisable title to the property and can raise finance secured over the property.

The docket transfer is a transfer narrated on the back of the Certificate of Confirmation related to the property or land being transferred. It is usually registered in the Books of Council and Session. It will not affect either the Sasines Register or the Land Register. This means that the recipient will have an uninfeft title. Should the recipient wish to raise finance over the property, additional conveyancing will be required at that time to give them an infeft title over which security can be placed.

This is the cheaper option at the time of administration of the estate but will likely cost more in the long run if it is likely that the recipient will wish to release equity from the property while retaining the property and the property needs to be registered in the Land Register to do so at that time.

Personal Effects

These can either be transferred or sold. In some cases, depending on the nature of the assets (or their age!), any personal effects that are not selected by beneficiaries, will need to simply be disposed of without any benefit, for example, where the furniture does not meet current health and safety standards.

Auction houses can usually either offer house clearance services if the property requires to be cleared or they will be able to advise of local contacts who will offer this service. You may also wish to consider local charities such as the British Heart Foundation or DEFRA who offer house clearance services. However you will be unlikely to receive any money for the items that are taken by the charities and therefore your Executors need to be mindful of their obligation to maximise the estate before choosing a charity to clear the property.

Vehicles

A vehicle can be transferred by signing the transfer slip on the V5. If you do not have the V5 for the vehicle, you will need to obtain a new one from the DVLA before title to the vehicle can be transferred[63].

If you sell or transfer the vehicle, you will need to apply to have any unused paid for vehicle tax refunded[64]. The vehicle tax no longer transfers

63 https://www.gov.uk/vehicle-log-book

64 https://www.gov.uk/vehicle-tax-refund

to the new owner. Likewise, the new owner will also need to tax the vehicle on transfer.

Yachts, Boats and Ships

To transfer the title to a UK registered yacht, boat or ship, the Executors must supply a signed Bill of Sale and register the title with the UK Ship Register. This can be done online[65]. If the yacht, boat or ship is registered abroad, the transfer will need to comply with the registration requirements of the country in which the yacht, boat or ship is registered.

Bank & Building Society accounts

The balances received on closure of bank and building society accounts will almost never be the same value that you were told was in the accounts at date of death. This can be for a variety of reasons such as interest (such as these accounts are currently providing!), credits such as state pension and automated payments such as direct debits and standing orders which have been received/paid post death but prior to the accounts being frozen. The funeral account may also have been settled from the account. If the deceased had debts with the bank/building society such as credit cards or loans, these may also have been settled from the balances on the accounts prior to the funds being sent to you. You should therefore always ask for statements covering the period from date of death to date of closure of the account in order to reconcile the funds received. This will also give you the opportunity to ascertain if there are any other assets or debts that have not otherwise been identified eg a standing order crediting from an unknown bank account or a credit from a personal pension.

National Savings & Investments

Premium Bonds can be left in the prize draw for up to a year after the death. There is an option on the encashment form to defer encashment

---

65 https://www.gov.uk/register-a-boat/the-uk-ship-register

until after the one-year anniversary expires. On the expiry of the one-year anniversary, NSI will automatically redeem the premium bonds and any associated prizes and remit them by bank transfer or warrant (like a cheque) payable to the Executor or any other previously specified person.

Any other asset held with NSI can simply be transferred or encashed as you would do with any other bank account. No deferment period for encashment applies to these products.

Publicly Listed Shares

Where shares are held by a registrar such as Equiniti, Computershare or Link Asset Services, the registrar will normally offer a postal share dealing service which will enable the shares to be sold or transferred. The forms will normally be sent to you when they reply to your initial enquiry. If the shares are in electronic format, that is to say, you receive a statement rather than a share certificate, you will only need the transfer/sale form with the Certificate of Confirmation to sell/transfer the shares.

If the shares remain in certificated format, you will need the share certificates as well as the Certificate of Confirmation to sell or transfer the shares. In the event that you do not have a share certificate for the full holding, you will need to complete an indemnity which the registrar will provide you with for the missing share certificates. There will be a fee to pay for this service which the registrar will advise of which will be payable at the time of the application. The fee will depend on the amount and value of the shares.

Where a postal sale or transfer service is not offered for a listed company, you will need to instruct a stock broker to deal with this matter on your behalf. This is the time to make friends with your local friendly broker as not all investment houses will do this for you, particularly if the transaction value is relatively low and there was no previous connection between the deceased and the investment house.

Private Company Shares

It is common in private companies for there to be restrictions on who can receive shares. There are usually offer round provisions contained in the founding documents of the company. This may mean that before the shares can be transferred or sold, the shares need to be offered to directors, other shareholders, persons holding a specific office within the company etc. Where those persons fail to take up the shares, the documents may allow for the transfer/sale to follow the terms of the Will or will otherwise detail how the disposal of shares should be dealt with.

These foundation documents can be found on Companies House under Incorporation documents.

TIP – when drafting a Will which involves shares in private companies, check the incorporation documents at Companies House to confirm that the person(s)/organisations that your Testator wishes to inherit the shares can in fact do so.

Life Policies

Life policies will either be paid immediately upon exhibition of the death certificate or may require a claim form to be completed before the proceeds can be paid. There will usually be an element of interest which is payable on life policies which will be payable on the time between the date of death and date of settlement of the claim. You will need to check whether this interest is paid net or gross of interest and where it has been paid gross of tax, report and pay the income tax due on the interest as part of the administration of the estate.

Bonds

Bonds can either be encashed or transferred. If the last surviving life assured was the deceased, the bond will come to an end on the notification of the death and the only option will be for the Executors to take the cash.

Ensure your Executors take financial advice before either encashing or transferring a bond that does not terminate on the death of the deceased as a chargeable event may be triggered which will affect the tax position of the estate and could result in the beneficiaries receiving less than they might otherwise have done had other action been taken (see Chapter 17 for further information)

State Benefits

Any sums due to the estate from the Department of Work and Pensions will usually be paid direct to a nominated bank account on completion of a form which will be supplied by the Department of Work and Pensions for the Executors to complete.

Personal pensions

Normally death benefits will be payable outwith the estate[66] and will not concern the Executors. There will however be times where there may be some drawdown of pension which will be payable to the estate. This will normally be paid upon completion of a claim form or a letter signed by the Executors directing how the funds should be paid.

HMRC

Any refund of tax that is due to the deceased, will normally be issued by cheque by HMRC made payable to the Executors. HMRC may send this directly to the Executor or to the person who completed the tell us once

66 Please note that the October 2024 budget has introduced changes to the pension regime expected to come into force in April 2027 which brings private pensions into the Inheritance Tax arena. At the time of writing this book, we do not have draft legislation to advise how this will work in practice. Therefore if you are dealing with estates involving pensions after the publication of this book, please review the legislation position in connection with pensions to ensure that the pension is treated appropriately for Inheritance Tax purposes.

service or they may send onto you. HMRC will also pay into an account nominated by the Executors on completion of a self-assessment tax return. If the person receiving the cheque from HMRC is a beneficiary of the estate, if they receive the cheque directly, it may be easier for them simply to encash the cheque and it be treated as a payment to account of their overall entitlement from the estate.

Refunds

Refunds can either be collected by completion of a claim form or written directions by the executor to the asset holder on where funds should be paid.

Foreign assets

Foreign assets come with their own unique set of additional requirements to transfer or sell the assets.

Where you have foreign shares, you may have to go through a somewhat torturous process of obtaining a medallion guarantee, particularly for shares held in the USA. A medallion guarantee is a special seal which will enable the foreign registrars to act on the transfer/sale instructions. It effectively is a seal given by a financial institution which guarantees the transaction to the registrars against a fraud. Very few financial institutions within the UK offer this service now. In reality, it is most commonly obtained by instructing one of the larger genealogist firms such as Title Research or Fraser & Fraser. You can expect the process of selling/transferring foreign shares to take around 6 months if not longer from start to finish. As soon as you realise that you have foreign assets involved in an estate, it would be advisable to instruct a firm in relation to obtaining the medallion guarantee as there are sometimes tight timescales involved in relation to when documents must be extracted to complete the transfer. You will usually require a certified extract of the Confirmation (with Will annexed) to accompany the transaction documents and therefore it should be ordered at the time of applying for

Confirmation. You may also require to obtain an Apostille from the Foreign and Commonwealth Office.

You may also have to obtain either a reseal of Confirmation or obtain a separate grant of Probate in the country that holds the foreign asset. In these circumstances, it would be wise to instruct local agents to undertake this work for you. Again, this should be instructed as early as possible into the administration process in order that you have time to ingather or trace relevant documents and understand the time constraints which may apply to overseas procedures.

There is an organisation called The Society of Trusts and Estates Practitioners (STEP). This is a global organisation of solicitors, accountants and financial professionals who specialise in private clients. If you are looking for a foreign contact to instruct, the STEP website has a search facility in which you can locate a relevant professional in a particular country[67]. This should give you a good starting point in instructing someone who knows what they are doing with estate administration in the relevant jurisdiction.

Memorandum of Appropriation

This is a Deed drafted by you and executed by the Executors with the consent of the appropriate beneficiary/beneficiaries which transfers assets to a beneficiary and enables the Executor to sell the asset as bare trustees for the beneficiary. This means that any Capital Gains Tax due on the sale of the asset will accrue to the beneficiary and not to the estate. Where there is a large gain, for example on the sale of a portfolio of shares, you should consider the use of this mechanism to reduce the overall amount of tax which would otherwise be payable by the estate were it to sell the

[67] https://www.step.org/directory/members

asset by enabling the use of multiple capital gains tax allowances from the beneficiaries compared to the single allowance that the Executors have[68].

68 The executors have a capital gains tax allowance for the first 3 tax years from death only – see chapter 18 on Capital Gains Tax for further information.

CHAPTER TEN

DISTRIBUTION, ACCOUNTS AND DISCHARGE

Payment of debts and expenses

Before you can distribute the estate to beneficiaries, you need to settle the outstanding debts on the estate.

Executors have 6 months from the date of death for creditors to intimate claims. The Executors would be well advised not to distribute the estate within the first 6 months of debt in case an otherwise unknown creditor comes to light. If this is the case and the Executors have already distributed the estate within that time frame, they will become personally liable to settle the debt.

There is a set order to the settlement of debts and expenses in an estate as follows:

1. Secured debts rank before any other debts and should be paid immediately upon realisation of the asset over which the debt is secured;

2. Privileged debts are paid before any other non-secured debts. These are debts of the deceased such as deathbed and reasonable funeral expenses (although they are not strictly debts in the traditional sense as funeral expenses cannot occur until someone has actually died!) and the expenses of administration of the estate;

3. Preferred debts have the next claim on the estate assets. These include items such as contributions to occupational pension schemes;

4. Ordinary debts are paid last and cover all other debts that are neither secured nor otherwise mentioned in the above sections.

Where the estate is found to be insolvent during the initial investigations, the outlays and remuneration of the interim/permanent trustee in sequestration must be settled after secured debts are paid but prior to the payment of privileged debts.

Order of Settlement of the Estate

Once the debts and expenses of the estate have been settled, you can then look to settle the estate with the beneficiaries. Again, there is a set order for the settlement of the estate with beneficiaries as follows:

1. Legacies – these are legacies of things such as a clock, granny's engagement ring etc and cash

2. Residue – this is a share of the residue of the estate, that is to say, everything that is left over after settlement of all debts, funeral expenses, taxes, legacies and administration expenses of the estate.

Specific legacies

Where the asset referred to in the Will cannot be found or is no longer owned by the deceased at the time of their death, the legacy will fail unless there is a contra indication in the Will that the beneficiary should receive some other item or share of the estate.

Specific legacies can be tricky where care has not been taken to sufficiently identify the item in question in the Will or where the deceased had multiple items which could fit the description.

A receipt from the beneficiary to acknowledge receipt should be sufficient discharge to the Executors in the exercise of their duties.

<u>**TIP**</u> – when drafting specific legacies in Wills, try to make the description sufficiently clear to enable identification of the item on death. If at all possible, get a photo of the item that can have the description of the item written on the back of it and store with the Will to aid identification eg this is the diamond ring being left to my niece, Josephine Bloggs under the terms of Clause 4f of my Will dated 3 April 2017.

Where the subject of a legacy cannot be located at the time of the death or has otherwise been sold or disposed of by the deceased before their death or was stolen, the legacy will adeem and nothing will be payable to the beneficiary from the estate in satisfaction of their legacy.

<u>Pecuniary Legacies</u>

Pecuniary legacies are cash legacies. Cash legacies should be paid before residuary bequests.

Where there are insufficient assets in the estate to settle the pecuniary legacies, the legacies will abate pro-rata to enable at least some of the legacies to be paid. Where abatement takes place, the residuary beneficiaries will receive nothing from the estate.

<u>Example</u>

A dies leaving an estate worth £10,000 with debts, funeral expenses and administration expenses of £7,500. This leaves a net estate of £2,500.

Under the terms of A's Will, they left legacies of £2,000 each to B and C.

The estate does not have £4,000 to settle the legacies in full to each of B and C after settlement of the debts, funeral and administration expenses.

In this case, as the legacies are of equal amounts B and C will each receive £1,250 each (50% of £2,500) and the legacies will exhaust the estate. Nothing will therefore be payable to the residuary beneficiaries.

Example

A dies leaving an estate per the terms of the example above.

Under the terms of A's Will this time, they left legacies of £1,000 to B and £3,000 to C.

Again, the estate does not have £4,000 to settle the legacies in full to each of B and C.

In this case, the legatees will receive the following:

B = £1,000

-------------------- x £2,500 = £625

(£1,000 + £3,000)

C = £3,000

-------------------- x £2,500 = £1,875

(£1,000 + £3,000)

Again, the residuary beneficiaries will receive nothing from the estate as the legacies have exhausted the estate.

Residue

The residue of the estate is the last to be paid after settlement of all funeral expenses, debts, legacies, taxes and expenses of administration of the estate. I normally find that this is paid to beneficiaries in a couple of instalments as payments to account as assets are ingathered before the final payment is made on approval of the accounts due to the amount of assets involved in my estates. As a firm, you should not want to hold onto funds for any longer than is necessary, particularly if your client account is non-interest bearing. Providing payments to account (reserving funds to meet your fees and any other anticipated expenses and taxes) also assists with maintaining relations with your beneficiaries as they can see progress being made in concluding the estate.

Transfer of Assets

Where the beneficiaries would wish assets transferred to them in lieu of them being sold and there is insufficient cash within the estate to meet all of the debts, taxes and expenses of administration of the estate, it will be necessary for the beneficiary to introduce the shortfall to the estate caused by them choosing to acquire the asset rather than having it sold prior to the transfers of assets being undertaken.

Purchase of Assets by a Beneficiary

It is possible for a beneficiary to purchase an asset from the estate. Most commonly, offers to purchase assets will be in relation to the deceased's house. The Executors are under a duty to maximise the value of the estate for the beneficiaries. In circumstances where an offer to purchase an asset from a beneficiary is received, you will need to consider the pros and cons of the acceptance of the offer versus putting the property on the open market and seeing what offers are received.

You may find that the family are more than happy to receive an offer from a beneficiary at the date of death value or an enhanced value without placing the property on the market as this will save the estate the estate agency and marketing costs to sell the assets. They will also have some degree of certainty that the transaction will not fall through due to lack of funding thus avoiding incurring aborted sale fees.

Where there is any sort of dispute as to the sale price (or indeed which beneficiary should have the opportunity to purchase the property), the Executors should consider an open market sale where the beneficiary so wishing to acquire the property can have the opportunity to bid for the property and take their chances against others on the open market. Ultimately it will be for the Executors to decide which offer is accepted.

In these circumstances, they may not select the highest offer because a lower offer is a cash purchase compared to a mortgaged purchase which might take longer to sell or because the purchaser isn't caught in a chain.

Where a beneficiary is entitled to a share of the residue which comprises a share in the asset in question, but they wish to acquire the asset, they will not need to introduce the full sale price into the estate to acquire the asset – they will only require to introduce the difference between their share of the asset and the sale price.

<u>Example</u>

A is entitled to a one quarter share of the residue of the estate which comprises a property worth £200,000.

A wishes to purchase the property from the estate and a sale price is agreed with the executors/beneficiaries at £240,000.

A will only need to introduce £180,000 to acquire the property (three quarters of the sale price) as they are already entitled to one quarter of the value of the asset.

<u>Accounts</u>

It will be necessary to prepare account of the intromissions of the Executors for approval. There is a school of thought that suggests that accounts should be prepared at the end of the estate once everything has been ingathered. I prefer to draft the accounts as I am going along for the following reasons:

1. The capital schedule detailing the assets at date of death can be used to form the basis of the inventory of the estate for Confirmation;

2. You can see problems in cash flow before they arise either for settlement of debts, expenses and taxes or in terms of whether assets should be transferred to beneficiaries or be sold;

3. You can see what income has arisen in the tax year to be able to prepare R185es;

4. You can see whether you have a capital gains tax issue and either take action to reduce the gain or register the estate in time to prepare self assessment returns.

The purpose of accounts is to show what has happened with the deceased's assets and to illustrate how the estate has been divided among beneficiaries. These accounts should detail the following:

1. Assets at date of death
2. Additional estate found post Confirmation
3. Sundry receipts
4. Income
5. Legacies
6. Expenses of administration
7. Division of the residue

There are various types of accounts that can be prepared as follows:

1. Statement of receipt and payments
2. Charge and discharge account
3. Schedular account

The choice is yours as to which style of accounting will be most suitable for your practice or estate. There is really no right or wrong option although I have provided my thoughts below on when each type of account may be suitable depending on what has happened in the estate.

Statement of Receipts and Payments

This is (in my humble opinion) really only suitable for very small estates where there are only a few transactions. This type of account consists of three sections:

1. Credits
2. Debits
3. Division of residue

It is basically a replication of the credits and debits from your cash ledger.

It is unlikely to help you identify whether there is any tax to pay for the period of administration of the estate. See Appendix One for an example style.

Account of Charge and Discharge

This might be considered to be the traditional way of preparing accounts for an estate and is a step further than the Statement of Receipts and Payments. It can be used for both small and large estates.

It is effectively a summary of all credit and debits and ensures that the credit side equals the debit side.

See Appendix Two for an example style.

Schedular account

I find that this account is the easiest account style to use to ensure that you don't miss anything tax wise during the administration of the estate. It sets out each individual component of the estate on a separate page thus making it easier to ascertain if an income tax liability has arisen and in what tax year and also whether capital gains tax will be an issue. It will also help you identify if a beneficiary needs to introduce funds into the estate to balance off their share of their estate and expenses of administration. It will also let you see if payments to account of residue could and should be made.

It can also be expanded to include Schemes of Division and personal statements where assets have been sold as bare trustees following a Memorandum of Appropriation being entered into. See Appendix Three for an example.

Discharge

Once the accounts have been prepared, they should be sent to the Executor(s) for approval prior to final distribution to the beneficiaries. It is competent to either have all Executors sign a single set of accounts or have each Executor sign an individual set of accounts and keep all signed copies together in the executry records. I normally send a duplicate set of accounts to the Executors to retain for their records.

Once the Executors have approved the accounts, a copy should be circulated to the residuary beneficiaries to approve and discharge the Executor of their duties before final payment is made. Again, I normally include a duplicate set of accounts for the beneficiaries retention.

Styles of approval and discharge can be found at https://www.lawscot.org.uk/members/rules-and-guidance/rules-and-guidance/section-e/division-d/guidance/executry-and-trust-accounting/

Where there is power in the Will to pay to a minor or guardian or any other person having control over someone who lacks legal capacity, the discharge should be modified to include the capacity in which the person is signing eg as parent, guardian, intervenor etc of the beneficiary.

CHAPTER ELEVEN

LEGAL RIGHTS

In Scotland, irrespective of the terms of your Will, certain individuals are entitled by law to a share of your estate after your death, known as their legal rights. This is because as Scots Law currently stands, it does not allow a spouse, civil partner or child to be wholly excluded from benefit. A civil partner is not the same as the cohabitant – a civil partnership is a formally registered relationship[69]. Cohabitant partners are not entitled to legal rights. The issue of legal rights above all else is the matter most likely to shock a family and cause a family fall out, in particular with a surviving spouse who is otherwise expecting the full estate to come to them (or indeed needs the full estate to come to them to maintain their standard of living).

Who can claim?

Legal rights only apply to the following categories of beneficiary:

1. The spouse/civil partner of the deceased (unless they have signed an agreement waiving their entitlement);

2. Children, including adopted or illegitimate children, but not including stepchildren; and/or

3. The children or remoter issue of a child who has died before the person who made the Will/died intestate

Legal rights do not have to be claimed – the parties can choose to accept the terms of the Will and sign a formal disclaimer discharging their legal rights. They may choose to do this because the Will gives them a better

[69] Civil Partnership (Scotland) Act 2004 as amended.

entitlement or because they wish to stand by the deceased's wishes rather than invoke the law. In addition, by claiming their legal rights, they will reduce the entitlement of beneficiaries in the Will and they may not wish to do this.

It is not possible to claim both legal rights and the entitlement under the Will – claimants must choose one or the other.

If the deceased is survived by a spouse/civil partner and children (or issue of a predeceasing child), the potential claim is as follows:-

- Spouse/Civil Partner – one third of the net moveable estate.
- Children (including issue of a predeceasing child of the deceased) – one third of the net moveable estate between them *per stirpes*.

If the deceased is survived by only a spouse/civil partner, or only children, that spouse or the children (including issue of a predeceasing child of the deceased) can claim one half of the net moveable estate. In the case of children, this is one half split between them so, if there were two children, they could claim one quarter each, three children would get one sixth each and so on.

Where a child has predeceased the deceased leaving children of their own, those children will share equally in the share that would have been attributable to their parent if in life.

Example

A dies leaving a spouse B and three children C, D and E. E predeceased his parent leaving two children of his own F and G.

The legal rights division is as follows:

- B – one third of the net moveable share.

- C – one nineth of the net moveable estate (one third divided by the 3 children C, D & E)

- D – one nineth of the net moveable estate

- E – one nineth of the net moveable estate with representation by issue therefore E's share passes as follows:

    - F – 50% of one nineth of the net moveable estate

    - G – 50% of one nineth of the net moveable estate

<u>How is the claim calculated?</u>

Legal rights can only be claimed on the deceased's net moveable estate, that is to say, the deceased's entire estate except land or buildings. The home is therefore not included in the calculation but money in the bank, investments, life policies, business interests etc, is included.

Exceptions to land and buildings not being included for legal rights calculations are as follows:

1. where there is land and/or buildings contained in a business. Depending on the way that the title to the land is held and the way it is included in the accounts of the business can mean that the land and buildings forms part of the business. As interests in business are moveable for the purposes of legal rights (be that as shares in a company, partnership share or sole trader), the inclusion of land and buildings as a moveable asset can significantly inflate the level of legal rights claims in an estate. This can commonly arise where land is involved in a partnership, and in particular, in the way in which land is held in Farming businesses. Identifying whether this is an issue for your estate will require the assistance of the deceased's accountant; and/or

2. Where missives to sell land are concluded prior to the death but the death occurred before settlement was able to take place.

Once the moveable estate has been identified, the net moveable estate is calculated by reference to the total of the estate at date of death, less funeral costs, less moveable expenses, less allowable expenses up to the Grant of Confirmation.

What is a moveable expense?

A moveable expense is an expense which is not secured over a property. A mortgage therefore cannot be deducted from the moveable estate to reduce the claim to legal rights.

For these purposes, funeral expenses including extras such as headstone, flowers etc are a deductible moveable expense although they could obviously not arise until the death occurred. Any tax due at the time of death including inheritance tax (pro-rated to the moveable estate only) can also be deducted.

Allowable expenses

Expenses to obtain Confirmation can also be included. This includes not just the Court fees but legal fees, fees for valuations of assets at the date of death and death certificates.

How long does a legal rights claimant have to make a claim?

Legal rights claimants have 20 years to claim or discharge their legal rights. In most cases, legal rights claimants will know if they are going to claim or discharge their entitlement once they are notified of their entitlement. However, there can be circumstances where this will not be possible, for example, in the case of a family fall out whereby it is necessary to search for a claimant. Family fall outs can also result in a legal rights claimant simply refusing to provide a decision for no other reason than to cause delays to the estate administration or to cause angst to the other family members who would be entitled to legal rights or any other share of the estate which cannot be paid out due to the claimant's indecision.

Minor Beneficiaries

Another case where legal rights decisions may not be capable of being executed in a timely manner is where there are one or more potential claimants who are minors. For the purposes of claiming or discharging legal rights, the age of legal capacity is 16 years old. However, it is possible for transactions made between the ages of 16-18 years old to be set aside by the courts if it is a transaction which is deemed to be prejudicial[70]. Under the circumstances, it is not advisable to accept a claim or discharge from a young person until they have attained the age of 18 years old. If the Executors do accept a claim or discharge prior to the beneficiary turning 18 years old, this could result in the Executors being out of pocket if the estate has otherwise been wound up eg there are insufficient funds to meet an entitlement under the Will where a legal rights discharge is over turned and the entitlement under the Will is greater than the legal rights claim. Given a beneficiary could be just a few hours, days or weeks old when the death occurs, this can cause a significant delay to the finalisation of the estate.

Interest

Interest accrues on the claim from the date of death until date of payment. There is no fixed interest amount which accrues on legal rights. It is usual to apply a rate of interest equal to the interest received by the Executors during the estate administration period if the estate has been manged prudently[71] eg if the Executors receive interest at 0.5% during

70 Age of Legal Capacity (Scotland) Act 1991 (c.50)

71 Kearon v Thomson's Trs 1949 SC 287

the administration of the estate, that rate should be applied to the legal rights calculation.

The Scottish Law Commission has suggested that interest in Legal Rights claims should be paid at a fixed rate. At the time of writing, this recommendation has not been implemented by the Scottish Government[72].

TIP – when drafting Wills, advise your clients of the existence of legal rights in order to manage expectations about who can and should inherit. The claiming of legal rights can substantially alter the division of the estate and can affect the financial security of both the spouse/civil partner and the children of the deceased.

TIP – where your testator has a business, it is worth while checking with their accountant whether any land will form part of the business and therefore be moveable for legal rights

Separation

It is important to note that married or civil partnership couples who are separated still have a claim to legal rights if one party dies before they have had the opportunity to divorce. Legal rights and indeed any right to claim in the other party's estate can however be discharged prior to divorce in the separation agreement. It is therefore important that you have sight of the separation agreement where the parties have not divorced to check if any legal rights or any other claim on the estate have been extinguished.

72 Scottish Law Commission Report on Succession. Paper no 215 – https://www.scotlawcom.gov.uk/files/7112/7989/7451/rep215.pdf

General

For more detailed information on legal rights, see "A Practical Guide to Legal Rights in Scotland" by S J MacDonald[73].

73 http://www.lawbriefpublishing.com/product/legalrightsinscotland/

CHAPTER TWELVE

COHABITING PARTNERS

For the purposes of succession in Scotland, a cohabiting partner does not have any automatic rights of succession.

Testate Estates

Where the deceased left a valid Will which excludes the cohabiting partner, that is the end of the matter. The cohabiting partner has no ability to make a claim on the estate and must rely on the good graces of those included in the Will to make provision for them. As you might imagine, this can lead to difficult situations such as the surviving partner being made to leave their house where the house was in the sole name of the now deceased partner. Likewise, where the deceased made a Will leaving limited provision for the cohabiting partner, that too will be the extent of what the partner can receive from the estate and there is no right of appeal or ability to petition the courts for additional provision.

Intestate Estates

Where there is no Will, the cohabiting partner has the ability to petition the courts within 6 months from the date of death for the same provision that they would have received had they been married/civil partners at the time of the death under s29 Family Law (Scotland) Act 2006[74]. This is a strict timeline which cannot at present be extended. A claim can be made by the surviving partner for provision provided that two conditions are met:

---

[74] S78 Trusts & Succession (Scotland) Act 2024 seeks to extend this time limit to 12 months. At the time of writing, this provision had yet to be brought into force.

1. before the death, the deceased was domiciled in Scotland; and

2. the deceased was cohabiting with their partner.

If the claim is successful, the surviving partner will receive:

1. a capital amount from the net estate; and/or

2. transfer of an asset(s) to them

A point to note here is that the net estate is calculated by reference to deducting Inheritance Tax, the ordinary debts and funeral expenses of the deceased and any claims to prior rights and legal rights that may exist for any surviving spouse/civil partner. You might think the latter point is odd but there are many people who separate from their spouses/civil partners, never formally divorce but move on to live with another person as partners. As long as neither spouse goes on to marry, they may not see the need to go to the expense of divorce, particularly where it was an amicable split.

Any such award cannot exceed the amount the surviving cohabitant would have received had they been married to the deceased at the time of their death. As far as the author is aware, at the time of writing this book, there have been no reported cases where a cohabiting partner has received the same amount that they would have received had they been married to the deceased. Each reported case where provision has been made has resulted in a lower award. If nothing else, this should assist in persuading future clients of the merits of having a Will!

As you will appreciate, 6 months is not a long time to establish who will be appointed as an Executor in order for the survivor to intimate a claim, never mind to raise the proceedings themselves. There is a way around this which is to simply intimate a claim against all known next of kin of the deceased but this is clunky and adds expense to the survivor's legal costs. If you are instructed to advise on a surviving cohabitant's rights in an estate, it is best to involve your litigation team at the earliest possible opportunity. Spouses/civil partners are significantly down the pecking order in terms of inheritance on intestacy where there are prior relatives, but it is safe to say that cohabitants are even further down that list of priority.

You need to remember when acting in an estate that you are acting for the Executor. You cannot therefore advise the cohabitant on their remedies for obtaining benefit from the estate. You can however suggest they take independent legal advice on their situation.

TIP – When acting for a cohabiting couple, be it in succession planning, conveyancing, business law or any other area of law, it always worthwhile pointing out the potential danger of an out-of-date Will or having no Will whatsoever.

See chapter 14 for possible conflict situations when dealing with cohabiting couples and children of the deceased.

CHAPTER THIRTEEN

DIVORCE AND DEATH

Given that the estimated rate of divorce in the UK is 42%[75], it is safe to say that you are going to come across a deceased who is separated or divorced at least once in your career. Separation and divorce can affect how an estate is dealt with and importantly, it can affect a testator's wishes concerning who inherits what from the estate.

Succession (Scotland) Act 2016

Prior to the Succession (Scotland) Act 2016, divorce did not affect testate cases. Therefore if your deceased wrote a Will in 2005 leaving everything to their spouse, divorced their spouse in 2012 and died in 2014, that now divorced spouse would still inherit their entitlement under the terms of the Will which may not have been what the deceased wanted. In intestate cases, the surviving party to the divorce was no longer entitled to make any claim on the estate of their former spouse other than enforcing any alimentary financial arrangements which were governed by the terms of their financial settlement on divorce against their former spouse's Executors.

Following the introduction of the Succession (Scotland) Act 2016, the position regarding death and divorce changed. From 1 November 2016, the former spouse or civil partner is treated as having predeceased the deceased as long as the following conditions are met:

1. The deceased was domiciled in Scotland after 1 November 2016; and

[75] "UK divorce statistics will give you cold feet" 21 September 2021, www.dontdisappoint.me.uk

2. The divorce must have been obtained in Scotland, England, Wales, Northern Ireland, the Channel Islands, the Isle of Man or otherwise is a divorce which is legally recognised in Scotland.

This means that the failsafe provisions in the Will will operate in place of the spouse. Where there are no failsafe provisions or the failsafes have failed to survive the deceased, the laws of intestacy will take over. The surviving former spouse or civil partner will also have no claim at this stage as they are not a category of beneficiary who can claim under intestacy law.

There may be situations whereby a person may wish their former spouse or civil partner to continue to benefit from their estate. In that situation, it will be necessary for the person to grant a new Will which expresses the assets or share of the estate that should intentionally pass to the former spouse or civil partner eg I leave my interest in the property known as 8 Acacia Avenue, Appletown to my former wife X residing at Y notwithstanding our divorce.

Executors, Trustees and Guardians

Following the Succession (Scotland) Act 2016, an appointment of a former spouse or civil partner as Executor and/or Trustee under the terms of a Will will automatically fail unless there is a stated intention to the contrary.

This is not without its complications, particularly where there are children of the relationship involved. Where the estate is passing to children, the deceased may well wish their former spouse or civil partner to be involved in an administrative capacity to assist with managing the funds for their joint children. In addition, they may also wish to have their former spouse or civil partner look after their joint minor children (or indeed the converse) and therefore it is important that these matters are covered off prior to the death with the divorcing parties.

Survivorship Destinations

Divorce also did not affect survivorship destinations (also called special destinations) in property titles. If survivorship destinations were not evacuated by the divorcing parties during proceedings, then on the death of one of the parties, the title would pass automatically to the survivor of them, regardless of what was written in the Will or how the estate devolved on intestacy or indeed what should happen under the terms of any financial settlement agreement on divorce.

In 2006, the law was amended to revoke survivorship destinations in property titles. The effect of the change is that on divorce, the survivorship destination in the titles dissolves and each party holds their share of the property free of the other party and therefore can bequeath their share of the property to anyone. This is not without its own complications as the surviving former spouse or civil partner could then find themselves owning the property with much hated former in-laws. If the surviving spouse or civil partner is the resident party in the property, this can also mean that the new owner following the death could also take up residence in the property with the result that the former spouse or civil partner finds that their home is no longer theirs to do with at they wish. It is therefore really important when dealing with a divorced client to check whether they continue to own property with their former partner and try to resolve any potential problems regarding future ownership of the property on death before a death occurs.

The Succession (Scotland) Act 2016 extended the revocation of survivorship destinations to all assets, not just property eg on shares, investments etc.

TIP – if your firm deals with divorce, you should always ask to review the Will of the party you are acting for to make sure the Will still does what the testator wants in view of the changes to their circumstances.

CHAPTER FOURTEEN

PROBLEM EXECUTORS AND BENEFICIARIES

You will from time to time, come across problem Executors and beneficiaries. Now I'm not talking about those people who are annoyed that they have not received their inheritance today when Granny was only buried yesterday and are irate that there is a due process to go through (although you will certainly come across a fair few of these people over the course of your career!). In this case, I'm talking about the people who through by accident or design can bring the administration of an estate to a grinding halt.

Where the testator appoints an Executor in the Will, the Executor must do one of the following:

1. Accept their appointment and administer the estate;

2. Resign their appointment, for example where they have commenced with the administration of the estate but are unable to continue through to Confirmation eg because of ill health; or

3. Decline their appointment which means that they have not dealt in any way with the administration of the estate.

Where another solicitor or professional trust company has been appointed as Executor and it is desired by the beneficiaries/co-Executors that they do not administer the estate, it is a professional courtesy when writing to obtain the professional Executor's declinature, that you give them sufficient information to decline their appointment. By this, I mean confirming that there are no family disputes which would warrant the continued appointment of an independent party as an Executor or that the estate is a small estate or passes in full to a single beneficiary. Give the professional Executor the reasons why they should not accept their appointment. Do not assume that a professional Executor will automatically resign or decline their appointment. Most corporate Executors will have been appointed for a reason and will wish to consider whether they should accept or decline their appointment.

Executor Datives

It is important to note that an Executor Dative cannot resign office or assume another Executor to act. It therefore important that the person or people being appointed as Executor Dative are prepared to deal with the role for the long haul. If a change of Executor is required, for example, due to ill health, then the initial appointment will need to be recalled and a fresh petition lodged to have a new Executor appointed.

Death

Where an Executor dies before Confirmation is applied for, their death needs to be narrated in the declaration to the Confirmation application to prove why Confirmation should not be taken out in their name.

Where an Executor dies post Confirmation but prior to the estate being administered, you may need to obtain Confirmation ad non executa where the Executor who has died is the sole surviving Executor and there remains unadministered estate. This enables the Executors of the now deceased Executor to obtain Confirmation to the estate of the original deceased and sit in their shoes.

Foreign Executor

A foreign address for an Executor will not affect their ability to obtain Confirmation. What it can do however is add a time delay and in certain cases, additional expense to the administration of an estate where time sensitive documents need to be couriered abroad as there will be documents where a wet signature is required to progress the administration of the estate or ingather the assets. In these circumstances, a foreign Executor may wish to decline or resign their appointment or perhaps assume a local Executor prior to resigning if they are the sole Executor nominate.

Where you have a foreign Executor who wishes to act, there are certain points which you need to consider:

Where you have a sole foreign Executor but they happen to be in the UK when the estate is ready to progress to Confirmation, they must physically sign the Confirmation paperwork;

Where you have a sole foreign Executor but they are not present in the UK when the estate is ready to progress to Confirmation, they can:

1. have the papers sent to them to sign (which is not without its own issues if you are sending original accompanying documents to be signed rather than registered extracts and they go missing);

2. grant a power of attorney in favour of someone who is resident in Scotland authorising the Attorney to sign the Confirmation application and obtain Confirmation in the name of the Executor. Styles for this documentation required for this procedure can be found in Currie on Confirmation[76]; or

3. where the Executor is resident in certain countries, a Consular Official can obtain Confirmation on behalf of the Executor Nominate where a Power of Attorney in favour of the Consular Official under s2 Consular Conventions Act 1949 is so granted. It is a condition of these provisions that the Executor has not granted a previous Power of Attorney in favour of anyone else. The powers invoked to a Consular Official extend further than those under the Power of Attorney procedure above and can include the ingathering of the estate where the Power of Attorney includes that power. As a Consular Official will likely charge for

76 9th edition, Scobbie, Eilidh

their services in this regard, one is left to wonder why a Consular Official would be anything other than a last choice when dealing with a foreign Executor.

Where there is more than one Executor, then the non-foreign Executor will be expected to sign the Confirmation application rather than the foreign Executor signing themselves or by their Attorney.

Where the estate is taxable or otherwise where there is a need for an IHT400 to be completed in respect of a non-taxable estate, the IHT400 will still need to be signed by the foreign Executor as an individual.

The power of attorney option for a foreign Executor will work regardless of whether the Executor is a nominate or dative appointment.

There is also a seldom used mechanism in relation to a foreign Executor of a judicial factor being appointed to administer the estate under the Act of Sederunt from 13 February 1730. This can only be used where the foreign Executor has not granted sufficient powers to another person to extract Confirmation on the Executor's behalf and is known as the appointment of a Factor loco absentis. This mechanism is very seldom used if for no other reason than with the advent of modern technology and international courier services, there are so many alternative cost effective and practical ways to obtain a speedy declinature, resignation, signature on documents or Power of Attorney from the foreign Executor. In addition, where a factor is involved, Caution will also need to be sought prior to Confirmation being obtained – even whether the estate is testate – which will add costs to the administration of the estate. It is therefore an option which should be very considered as a last resort.

Minor Executors

Minors are not capable of obtaining Confirmation due to their age. Where the minor is just a few months off reaching majority, you may wish to consider delaying the administration of the estate until they are capable of providing instructions.

Where delaying the administration of an estate is not a possibility, if the child has a legal representative, the legal representative can step in to deal with the administration of the estate on their behalf as qua legal representative. A legal representative for these purposes will be a person with parental rights[77]. This will usually be the genetic parents of the child or where the birth mother has acted as a surrogate but is married or in a civil partnership, the husband/civil partner will also have parental rights over the child until the adoption has taken place, notwithstanding they have no genetic connection to the child in question. Adoptive parents will also usually have been awarded parental rights as part of the adoption procedure. A legally appointed guardian will also be able to act as legal representative unless the power to assert parental rights has been revoked by the Court.

Where there are two or more persons with parental rights over the minor, each can act independently and without the consent of the other in respect of the estate. This could lead to clashes in the estate if conflicting instructions are given. You might enquire how someone might be entitled to act in the administration of the estate where there are two people with parental rights capable of acting. While it would be unusual, there could be situations where there are more than the two parents with parental rights, for example such as a grandmother who looks after the child and has been previously granted parental rights without the parents being stripped of their rights in court.

Where there is no legal representative for a minor (for example, it is the surviving parent who has died without making a guardianship appointment for their minor children), a petition can be made to the court to have a guardian appointed who would then be entitled to deal with the administration of the estate on behalf of the minor as Executor qua guardian.

---

77 S1(d) and S2(d) Children (Scotland) Act 1995

If there is the unfortunate position whereby there is no one available or willing to either exercise parental rights or be appointed as a guardian, then a commissary factor can be appointed to act as Executor qua factor. Caution will be required for the appointment. The initial writ containing the terms of the appointment must be served on the Accountant of Court and all known relatives of the child on both sides of the family. This will require a family tree to be built which may be difficult where there is no immediate family coming forward to claim the orphaned child/children and will no doubt involve the need to instruct a genealogy firm to confirm the extent of the child's relatives.

Cohabitant couples with children

Where there is a surviving cohabitant partner and the deceased died intestate, intimation of the surviving cohabitant's claim needs to be served on all relatives who would otherwise be entitled to the intestate estate. Where there are children of the couple, intimation of the claim would need to be served on the children of the deceased. As the children have a surviving parent in the form of the surviving cohabitant partner, this puts the cohabitant in a conflict of interest position as they will be attempting to protect their own financial position as well as the childrens', which could ultimately be at odds with one another. In these situations, the Court should be petitioned to appoint a curator ad litem to represent the childrens' interests in their deceased parent's estate where the children of the deceased are not adults who can instruct separate representation.

TIP – where dealing with a cohabitant couple in life, encourage them to make a Will to protect the interests both of the surviving partner and their children. The death of a loved one is difficult enough to deal with without the worry that the surviving parent may be made financially insecure if the petition to the Court does not provide that which the deceased person would have wished them to have.

Disappearance

Where an Executor goes missing or otherwise cannot be found from the outset, you will need to consider whether a tracing agent should be appointed to locate them or, if appropriate, confirm their death.

Criminal Convictions

There are only two instances whereby a criminal conviction can affect a person's ability to administer an estate as Executor as follows:

1. Where the Executor has a conviction for a financial crime such as embezzlement or fraud and Caution is required to obtain Confirmation, it is likely that most insurance houses will refuse to underwrite a Bond of Caution. Bearing in mind that the number of insurance houses offering Bonds of Caution is extremely limited, in these circumstances it may be wise for the Executor with the criminal conviction to resign or decline their appointment or where they are sole Executor, to assume someone else to act in their place.

2. Where the convicted criminal killed the deceased[78]. Being convicted of the crime does not necessarily prevent the convicted person from acting in the administration of the estate but it does

[78] S80 Trusts and Succession (Scotland) Act 2024 gives powers to the Sheriff to decline a petition to have someone appointed as Executor Dative of the deceased where they are either being prosecuted for (actively and the case has not yet resulted in the acquittal or dismissal of the case against the defendant) or have been convicted of the crime of killing the deceased, either in Scotland or any other jurisdiction (or the equivalent crime). Where a person regardless finds themselves appointed as Executor Dative in such circumstances, they can be removed as Executor Dative as being unfit for office under s7 and 8 Trusts and Succession (Scotland) Act 2024 from 26th June 2024.

certainly find its way to adding complexity into an estate, particularly in situations where Caution is required.

Ill-health

Where an Executor is suffering from ill-health which could affect their ability to administer the estate, for example, have frequent spells in hospital or are heading towards possible dementia, it would be appropriate in these circumstances to request the Executor to decline their appointment. Where they are the sole Executor, it would be helpful for the Executor to assume another person to act as Executor and then resign their appointment.

Where a dative appointment has been made and the ill-health occurs between the dative appointment and the application for Confirmation, the dative appointment can be recalled and a fresh motion lodged for a new Executor or in favour of the remaining Executors dative who are not in ill-health from the initial application.

Incapax Executors

Unlike the procedure where there is a foreign Executor, it is not competent for any other person to grant a Power of Attorney to deal with the wholesale administration of the estate. It is however competent for an Attorney to decline an appointment as Executor on behalf of an incapax Executor where the Power of Attorney has the appropriate powers to do so.

Where the Power of Attorney is either non-existent or contains insufficient powers to enable the Attorney to decline the role of Executor on behalf of the Granter, it is also possible for the Attorney (or a relative where there is no Attorney) to petition the court for a guardianship order (or in certain cases an intervention order) to deal with the administration of the estate. In these circumstances, the petitioner will be discerned Executor qua guardian to the estate.

That being said, there have been two recent in case law since 2023 which have sought to move the boundaries forward in respect of incapax Executors with decisions from what might be considered pragmatic Sheriffs:

1. In Gordon, Petitioner[79], the Will had appointed Executors and left the residue to the deceased's now incapax widow. Both Executors had predeceased the deceased. The widow was therefore entitled to act as Executor nominate under s3 Executors (Scotland) Act 1900. The widow had a Power of Attorney in place. The Attorney sought to be discerned as Executor Dative qua Attorney which was granted by extending the powers in the Adult with Incapacity (Scotland) Act 2000 which enables a guardian to be appointed as Executor Dative qua Guardian to Attorneys on the basis that both are supervised by the Office of the Public Guardian and the Court. There was also no public interest in delaying the administration of the estate. It is interesting to note that in this case, the petition was intimated on both the Office of the Public Guardian and the Lord Advocate but neither entered the case.

2. In Cornforth and Another, Petitioners[80], the deceased's wife was appointed as Executor under her late husband's Will but at the time of his death, was incapax with a Power of Attorney in place. In this case, the Attorney was discerned as Executor dative qua attorney of the incapax widow due to the following factors:

    a. The deceased's will have enabled substitute executors to be appointed and therefore delictus personae did not apply to the widow's appointment; and

79 2023 SLT (sh ct) 187

80 2024 SLT (sh ct) 27

b. The Sheriff considered that as the widow's Power of Attorney enabled the Attorney to act with "full power for me and in my name", there was no delegation of the role of Executor as the Executor was standing in the shoes of the widow and acting in her name.

With people living older and the increase in medical conditions affecting the brain such as dementia, this is likely to be an evolving area of law.

TIP – ensure your Power of Attorney styles contain the fullest possible powers for the Attorneys to act on behalf of the incapax adult and include a clause which enables the Attorney to resign, decline or accept office as Executor or trustee of an estate or trust where it is appropriate to do so.

S6 Trusts and Succession (Scotland) Act 2024 seeks to resolve the issue of incapax executors but at the time of writing this book, the provisions are not yet in force.

Where additional Executors have been appointed as well as the incapax Executor and it is not possible to obtain a declinature from the incapax's Attorney, it is competent for Confirmation to be taken out in the name of the capax Executors. In this scenario, a medical certificate confirming the incapax Executor's lack of capacity can be exhibited with the application for Confirmation. The declaration should also contain reference to the medical certificate and the Executor's incapacity.

Where the Executor becomes incapax post Confirmation, then there are three options to progress the administration of the estate;

1. Where there is a guardian for a sole incapax Executor, it is possible for an Eik to be taken out by the Guardian on behalf of the Executor;

2. Where there is more than one Executor, an Eik will only be granted in the names of the remaining Executors, once the incapax Executor has been formally removed by the Court;

3. A beneficiary can raise an action for a new Executor or Executors to be appointed where there is a sole incapax Executor without a guardian who can take forward the administration of the estate.

Minor Beneficiaries

Under Scots law, a person attains the age of legal capacity at age 16 years old. If there is no provision in the Will to extend the age, a child will inherit at age 16 years old. If the deceased dies while the child is still tiny, this can mean that the Executors have to retain and manage the funds for a significant number of years. Where there are no provisions for funds for a minor beneficiary to be held in trust, you will need to contact the Accountant in Court for directions on the administration of the funds until the minor comes of age where the value of the funds due to the child exceed £20,000.

CHAPTER FIFTEEN

VARYING THE TERMS OF AN ESTATE

It is possible to vary the terms of an estate. Varying an estate can take place for a number of reasons such as:

1. The beneficiary doesn't need or want all of their entitlement eg the acceptance of the entitlement in full or in part may either create an inheritance tax problem for the beneficiary or exacerbate an existing inheritance tax problem for the beneficiary

2. The beneficiary wants to honour wishes of the testator which were made known to the beneficiaries before the death but to which the testator had not been able to commit to writing before the death; or

3. to rectify a perceived wrong in the Will, for example, where there is a legacy of cash to all grandchildren that were alive at the time of the Will but there is another grandchild who has arrived into this world recently.

A variation can occur in a testate or intestate estate.

The question may therefore arise as to how best a beneficiary can vary their entitlement from an estate. While I would class a variation of the estate as part of personal estate planning, it is still important to know how best to deal with this as you may have a beneficiary come to you for general advice but you are not dealing with the estate or you may need to send the beneficiary to another firm if you are acting for the estate and find yourself conflicted.

Gifts

The beneficiary can simply gift their entitlement (or whatever part they wish to dispose of) to the new recipient after receipt. If this is done, this will be a Potentially Exempt Transfer (PET) and the donor will require to survive the transfer by 7 years for it to fall outwith their estate for inheritance tax purposes. I would normally only suggest this as an option where small amounts are being gifted, the proposed gifts fall within the relevant inheritance tax allowances or in the case of a bigger sum not covered by inheritance tax exemptions and reliefs, where there is a general expectation that the donor will reasonably survive for 7 or more years.

A gift can take place at any time but generally I would suggest that if the beneficiary (or indeed anyone thinking about making a gift at any time!) is going to make a gift, make it sooner rather than later to start the 7-year PET clock running. The longer the delay in making a gift, the longer the donor has to survive to get the gift out of your estate eg if a person decides to make a gift in 2024 but doesn't physically make the gift until say 2026, it will take until 2033 for it to be out of the beneficiary's estate. Had the gift been made in 2024, the gift would be out of the estate in 2031.

Deed of Variation

An alternative to gifts is for the beneficiary who wants to divest themselves of some or all of the estate to enter into a Deed of Variation (also known as a Deed of Family Arrangement). A Deed of Variation can be entered into in respect of a testate or intestate estate. A Deed of Variation is a formal written deed which has the effect of redirecting the terms of the Will or the intestacy to redirect the donor's share of the estate (or part share or a specific asset as the case may be) to the new beneficiary or beneficiaries.

The conditions for a Deed of Variation to work are as follows:

1. It must be entered into within 2 years of the date of death;

2. It must be in writing;

3. It must contain a declaration that the Deed is to be treated as a variation under s142 (1) Inheritance Tax Act 1984;

4. It must be signed by the donor;

5. It must not be made in exchange for any goods or benefits, for example entering into a Deed of Variation to give someone benefit in exchange for a return of cash other than allowing for the costs of the preparation of the deed to be met[81];

6. Where the variation is in favour of a charity or registered club, that charity or club has been given notice of the variation[82]; and

7. In situations where the terms of the Deed alters the inheritance tax treatment of the estate, it must be intimated to HMRC and any additional inheritance tax due must be paid along with interest (if appropriate)

The person in whose favour the variation is made does not need to be alive. Now this might seem to be a strange concept – why would you want to give a dead person something when they cannot use it? However this might be a useful concept where a husband and wife die in quick succession with an uneven ownership of assets with the first to die having the majority of assets. In this scenario, where the estate passes to a non exempt beneficiary such as their child, Inheritance Tax may be payable on the estate. If the second to dies assets are under the nil rate band and the child is also the beneficiary of the second estate, then the child may wish to vary their entitlement in the first estate in favour of the second to die to enable as much of the nil rate band to be used as possible in the

[81] S142(3) Inheritance Tax Act 1984 and S62(8) Taxation of Capital Gains Act 1992

[82] S142(3A) Inheritance Tax Act 1984

second person's estate and reduce the overall inheritance tax payable between the two estates.

Charities

Where a variation is in favour of a charity or registered club, the easiest way to prove that they have received notification of the variation is to have them counter sign the Deed. Where there are multiple parties, you might not want to risk circulating the principal deed and therefore you can show that you have intimated the Deed on the relevant parties by providing a copy of the letter sent to the parties to advise. These letters can be sent by recorded delivery and the delivery numbers provided as well to enable HMRC to look up the Royal Mail website to check that delivery has taken place.

Timescales

A Deed of Variation can be undertaken at any time in the two-year period from the date of death and will apply regardless of whether the assets remain unadministered within the estate or have been distributed in full or in part to the donor.

An important point to note is that a variation can only be undertaken once in connection with the asset/entitlement – it is therefore important that you get the terms correct and it is undertaken on time as it cannot be redone. This does not mean that you cannot have multiple beneficiaries varying their entitlement in a single estate, just that each beneficiary can only vary their individual entitlements once per estate[83].

Example

A wishes to vary a £10,000 legacy given to them under the Will of B. A varies the legacy by a Deed of Variation to pass it to C. A then changes

[83] See Russell V IRC (1988) STC 195

their mind before the legacy is paid from the estate and wishes the legacy to be divided between C and D. As it is the same asset in connection with the same death, a second variation is not possible. If however upon receipt of the £10,000 from B's estate, C then decides to gift half of it to D in implement of A's wishes, this is possible but this will be treated as a gift (PET) by C to D and will not be read back into the Will of B.

Effect

Another important point to note is that the Deed of Variation only works for Inheritance tax and succession law purposes. For Income Tax purposes, liability for any such tax due on the varied estates remains with the donor. This is particularly important if some or all of the assets are being varied into a trust as while the settlor of the trust for Inheritance Tax purposes will be considered to be the deceased, the income tax liability will arise on the beneficiary creating the trust through the variation and the Capital Gains Tax liability *may* follow the person varying[84]. Depending on the nature of the Variation, it can also be viewed as a voluntary divestment of assets by the donor for the purposes of assessment of care costs and other means tested benefits should the person varying their entitlement require a financial assessment or already be within the care regime. It is therefore important that the granter takes advice on what they are trying to achieve with the proposed variation.

Pitfall for the Unwary

All parties affected by the Deed of Variation must be capable of consenting to the variation. Minors and adults lacking capacity can prove to be problematic when it comes to varying an estate as they will be unable to consent to a variation of their share of the estate. This will not prohibit anyone else from varying their own individual share of the estate but can affect the ability to vary where the benefit is, for example, held

[84] See Marshall V Kerr [1995] 1 AC 148 and s68C Taxation of Capital Gains Act 1992

jointly with a person who lacks capacity or where there is a trust which needs varied but involves one or more persons who lack capacity. Where a variation is not possible, and one party still wishes to divest themselves of the asset, they are of course free to decline their share of the estate, assign their share or alternatively, receive the share of the estate and then gift it on (however the 7-year PET rules will apply rather than the preferential treatment of the variation which bypasses their estate completely).

Varying Mortis Causa Trusts

Where a trust is created in an estate which is not suitable for the circumstances, and there are minor beneficiaries which prevents a variation occurring, it should be possible for the trustees to use any powers granted by the trust deed to vary the entitlements and fix the trust. Any such amendment undertaken within 2 years of the date of death will be read back into the estate under s144 Inheritance Tax Act 1984.

Example

A dies leaving their house in trust for such of their grandchildren as attain the age of 17. At the time of death, all beneficiaries are under the age of 17. As such, the trust falls under the relevant property regime which denies the estate the ability to claim the residential enhancement to the nil rate band. The trustees have the power within the Will to advance the age at which the beneficiaries inherit. If the trustees elect to advance out the property into either bare trusts or interest in possession trusts for the beneficiaries within 2 years of the death, this will be read back into the estate and the "new" trust will enable the estate to qualify for the residential enhancement.

Confirmation

If the Deed of Variation is entered into before Confirmation is granted, the Deed of Variation needs to be referred to in the declaration to the Confirmation and docketed and exhibited as relative to the application. This also means that the terms of the variation will become a public record as they will be recorded in the Court Books. If the person varying the estate does not wish the terms of the variation to be made public, the Deed of Variation should not be entered into until after Confirmation has been granted. If you are likely to have a variation in an intestate estate which has not been entered into before applying for Confirmation, you should advise the insurers when taking out the Bond of Caution of the likelihood of the variation occurring.

Disclaimers & Renunciations

This is most likely to occur where there has been a family fall out and the intended beneficiary wants nothing from the deceased's estate. This is not however the only situation in which this can occur.

A disclaimer occurs in intestacy. A renunciation occurs in intestate estates. The effect of the renunciation or disclaimer is for the person granting it to give up their entitlement from the estate.

An effective disclaimer/renunciation must:-

1. disclaim all of the benefit left to the beneficiary. If only part of a benefit needs to be redirected and the granter wishes to retain some part of their entitlement, then a Deed of Variation would be the most appropriate mechanism to deploy;

2. the claimant cannot have derived any benefit from their share of the estate at the time the disclaimer is made;

3. the claimant cannot direct who should receive their share of the estate in substitution. Again, if the claimant wishes to control

who inherits their share of the estate, a Deed of Variation would be the most appropriate mechanism;

4. where Tax benefits are sought, the disclaimer must be in writing[85].

It is possible for any disclaimer/renunciation to be retracted however this can only occur where no one else has acted to their detriment following the disclaiming of the share of the estate. The fact that a disclaimer can be retracted illustrates further why it is best practice to get any disclaim of benefit committed to writing as then the Executors can prove the effective date for when the disclaim happened and can establish who has taken what action and the ramifications of it for all beneficiaries of the estate should the disclaimer change their mind at a later stage.

Differences between Deeds of Variation and Disclaimers/Renunciations

Disclaimer/Renunciation	**Deed of Variation**
Declines all benefit from the estate	Accepts the benefit from the estate then redirects some or all of it
Ineffective where a benefit has been derived from the share of the estate.	Can take effect regardless of whether a benefit has already been derived from the share of the estate.
Cannot direct who should benefit in substitution for the Disclaimer.	Can direct who should receive the varied entitlement and in what proportions.

85 See https://www.gov.uk/hmrc-internal-manuals/inheritance-tax-manual/ihtm35161 for further information.

Can be made at any time as long as the conditions are met.	Must take effect within two years of the date of death to be effective for Tax purposes.
Can be done orally or in writing.	Must be in writing only.
Qualifies for Section 142 (1) Inheritance Tax Act 1984 and Section 62 (6) Taxation Capital Gains Act 1992 relief but only when committed to writing.	Qualifies for Section 142 (1) Inheritance Tax Act 1984 and Section 62 (6) Taxation Capital Gains Act 1992 relief.

CHAPTER SIXTEEN

INHERITANCE TAX

This is the tax that is guaranteed to send both clients and practitioners around the bend! This book will only scratch the surface of what you will come across on the Inheritance Tax (IHT) arena but it should at least give you the basics to get to grips with the most frequent IHT issues that you are likely to come across. For a more thorough in depth look at IHT, look at Tolley's Inheritance Tax by Malcolm Gunn[86].

What is subject to inheritance tax?

Inheritance tax is payable on the net estate at date of death, that is to say the balance of assets left after all funeral expenses and allowable debts have been deducted. The amount of inheritance tax due can be reduced by deduction of applicable allowances and it can be increased by the addition of lifetime gifts.

The Basics

Nil Rate Band

The point at which IHT usually (key word here is usually!) becomes payable is when an estate exceeds the nil rate band (NRB) as set from time to time. The NRB at the time of writing this book is £325,000. It has remained static since 2009 and is not expected to rise before 2030 thanks to Rachel Reeves Budget in October 2024. Estate above that limit is subject to IHT at 40% unless there is an exemption or relief which applies. This should be your starting point for all estate transactions.

[86] This publication is updated annually.

The Transferable Nil Rate Band

This applies to married couples/civil partners and enables the unused portion of the first spouse/civil partner to die's NRB to be transferred to the second spouse/civil partner to die's estate to offset IHT on the second death. Inter vivos gifts, legacies to non exempt beneficiaries and claims for legitim in the first estate can reduce the amount of the NRB that is available to transfer to the survivor's estate. Completion of Form IHT402 will assist with calculating the TNRB[87]. The Executors have 2 years from the date of death to make a claim for this relief.

Residential Enhancement to the NRB

The Residential Enhancement to the NRB or Residence Nil Rate Band (RNRB or RENRB for short) was introduced to extend the NRB where a qualifying residential interest is passed to lineal descendants on a death. It does not apply to Potentially Exempt Transfers (successful or failed) or Chargeable Lifetime Transfers. It only applies to the IHT due on estate assets.

A qualifying residential interest is an interest in a dwelling house which has been the deceased's residence. If the deceased owns two or more residential dwelling house interests at death, their Executors may elect only one to become the qualifying residential interest. Confusingly, the legislation was extended to enable the RNRB to be used where the deceased had owned a property at some point in their lives but no longer owned a property at the time of their death – for example, because they had moved into permanent residential care and their house had been sold to fund their care. This means that where the latter situation applies, you will need to track down records of the disposal to be able to calculate the application of the RNRB to the estate.

---

87 https://www.gov.uk/government/publications/inheritance-tax-claim-to-transfer-unused-nil-rate-band-iht402

Lineal descendants for the purposes of RNRB are classed as:

1. Children of the deceased;
2. Adopted children of the deceased;
3. Foster children of the deceased;
4. Any child to whom the deceased was appointed as a Guardian; and
5. Children and remoter issue of any of the above categories

You will notice that this includes categories of person who do not normally get a look in for succession law purposes or indeed for any other familial IHT exemption.

The RNRB, much like the NRB, is capable of revision by Parliament. Unlike the NRB, it has moved several times since 2017 as follows:

1. For deaths on or after 6 April 2017 – £100,000
2. For deaths occurring in the tax year 2018/19 – £125,000
3. For deaths occurring in the tax year 2019/20 – £150,000
4. For deaths occurring on or after 6 April 2020 – £175,000

The RNRB only applies to estates under £2m. It tapers off up to estates over £2.2m. Estates above £2.2m do not qualify for the relief.

While normally there must be a gift of the qualifying residential interest to a lineal descendant outright for the Residential Enhancement, it will also apply where the lineal descendant is a beneficiary of a trust set up on the death of the deceased which falls into one of the following categories and of which the qualifying residential interest is an asset:

1. Immediate post death interest in possession trust (IPDI);

2. Disabled persons trust;

3. Trust for bereaved minors; or

4. 18–25 Trusts

It is important to note that a disposal into a discretionary trust on death will **not** apply to benefit from the RNRB. This is a particularly important as a significant number of older Wills still carry a discretionary nil rate band trust clause within them. This was a tax planning mechanism deployed before the advent of the transferable nil rate band which enabled the nil rate band of the first spouse to die to be utilised in full or in part in situations where it would otherwise have been lost by passing the estate in full to the surviving spouse.

Unlike many other IHT reliefs and exemptions, you do not need to be married to take advantage of this relief but you do need to have a qualifying lineal descendent and either have a qualifying property or qualify under the downsizing rules.

Completion of Form IHT435[88] will assist with the calculation of the RNRB.

TIP – It is well worth reviewing your Will bank every 3 years or so. This will enable you to remind clients that they have made a Will (with you!). It also allows outdated tax planning in Wills to be revised as well as ensuring that the client's Will remains up to date taking account of their family circumstances.

88 https://www.gov.uk/guidance/claim-the-residence-nil-rate-band

The Transferable RNRB

As with the TNRB, the balance of unused RNRB is transferable to the estate of the surviving spouse or civil partner. Where the first death occurs prior to 6 April 2017, you can still transfer their allowance even though it did not apply at the time of their death. It can also apply where the property the transferable RNRB (TRNRB) applies to is not the same property that the first to die and the current deceased resided in together. As the first to die could not have used any of their RNRB if they died before 6 April 2017, 100% of their RNRB will be available to transfer to the survivor.

The TRNRB is based on a percentage basis. This means that you will need to calculate the unused portion of the first to die's RNRB. This is done as follows:

$$\frac{\text{Unused portion of the first to die's RNRB}}{\text{The RNRB applicable at the date of the first to die's death}} \times 100\%$$

You then multiply that percentage by the applicable RNRB at the time of the second to die's death and that will give you the available TRNRB.

It is worth noting that the maximum TRNRB is 100%. This means that if the deceased has been widowed twice, their executors can only claim TRNRB up to 100% of the value of the RNRB applicable at the time of the second to die.

Example

A marries B in 2002. B dies in 2005.

A marries C in 2009. C dies in 2016

A dies in 2021 when the RNRB is £175,000.

A's Executors wish to claim the TRNRB.

As both B and C died before 6 April 2017, 100% of their RNRB is available to transfer to A's estate.

A's Executor's can only claim £175,000 as the TRNRB. They can choose whether to use B or C's estate to transfer the RNRB.

Example

A marries B in April 2018. B dies in January 2019. B's executors used 75% of his RNRB.

A marries C in December 2019. C dies in May 2020. C's Executors used 25% of his RNRB.

A dies in 2021 when the RNRB is £175,000.

A's Executors wish to claim the TRNRB.

A's Executors can claim 25% of the unused TRNRB from B's estate (100% – 75% used on B's death) and 75% of the unused TRNRB from C's estate (100% – 25% used on C's death) thus enabling A's Executors to claim 100% TRNRB.

Had B's Executors used 90% of his RNRB, then A's Executors would only be able to claim 10% TRNRB from B's estate which when combined with the 75% available from C's estate would give A's Executors a maximum claim to the TRNRB of 85%.

Completion of Form IHT436[89] will assist with the calculation of the TRNRB.

89 https://www.gov.uk/government/publications/claim-to-transfer-any-unused-residence-nil-rate-band-iht436

The Executors have 2 years from the date of death to make a claim for this relief.

Downsizing Relief

This is a particular relief designed to let an estate take advantage of the RENRB that would have applied to the estate had the deceased not sold the qualifying property.

To qualify, the deceased must have:

1. Sold their home on or after 8 July 2015;

2. Bought a different property or moved into a care;

3. The original property would have qualified for the RENRB had it still been held at the date of death; and

4. The property is passing to lineal descendants

The Executors have 2 years from the date of death to make a claim for this relief.

Lifetime Gifts

Once your initial investigations are complete, you will have ascertained the value of the estate. In addition, you will need to ascertain what gifts the deceased made in the 7 years preceding the death (and in some cases the 14 years preceding death but more of that later!) as these can affect the total IHT which will be payable by the estate. It is important that questions regarding gifts are asked of Executors and close family as HMRC can charge up to 100% of the tax due on non-declared gifts as a penalty in addition to the actual tax that falls due[90]. It is also worth

[90] Hutchings V HMRC [2015] UKFTT 9 (TC) – case in which HMRC discovered a significant gift made by the deceased to his son through an offshore account via an anonymous tip off which the son had failed to

looking at bank statements to see if you can identify any gifts. Standing orders to family members will normally be at least indicative of a gift with the onus on the recipient to prove it was not a gift e.g. they can prove its payment for a subscription for the deceased, weekly shopping for the deceased etc. Cheques can also be another source of gifts. You can ask the bank to provide copies of the fronts of cheques that you suspect may be gifts.

There are different types of gifts that you need to be aware of when looking at estates. For these purposes, a gift can be anything. It can be cash, property, investments, jewellery and other personal effects or even a share in a business. The person gifting the asset is known as the donor and the person receiving the gift is known as the donee.

Particular care needs to be given where assets are sold at undervalue in a non-arm's length transaction as the difference between the sale price and the market value of the asset will also be classed as a gift.

Example

A owns a house. A wishes to downsize and their child B wishes to get a foot on the property ladder. A sells the house off market to B for £300,000. The actual open market value of the property at the time of sale is worth £400,000. Regardless of the fact that A has received cash in exchange for the asset, the gift element of the transaction is the £100,000 discount on the sale price.

---

declare to the solicitors handling the estate. The tax assessed as due on the gift was over £100,000 for which a penalty of 50% of the tax due was applied. The son appealed the decision blaming grief for forgetting about the gift. Had the Executors not written the letter, it is likely that the Executors would have been found personally liable for the penalty and the solicitors advising the Executors would have been looking at a negligence claim.

As IHT is not straightforward, there are different types of gifts that you can come across when dealing with an estate.

Potentially Exempt Transfer otherwise known as a PET

PETs are gifts made to an individual. PETs are exempt from IHT regardless of value if the person making the gift survives the date of gift by 7 years. Note that the 7-year clock for gifts does not start until the funds or asset have left the donor so the clock for gifts made by cheque will not start ticking until the recipient has banked the cheque and it has cleared the donor's account or the asset e.g. a painting, jewellery etc has left the possession of the donor.

Failed Potentially Exempt Transfer otherwise known as a Failed PET

This is where the donor fails to survive the gift by 7 years. In this case, the failed PETs have the first bite of the cherry so to speak in respect of the NRB applicable at the time of the deceased's death which can alter the ultimate division of the estate.

Example

Mrs A makes the following capital gifts:

- £100,000 to her niece Miss B on 25 September 2020
- £50,000 to her nephew Mr C on 6 April 2019
- £25,000 to her goddaughter, Ms D on 12 May 2002

Mrs A dies on 30 June 2021 with a nil rate band of £325,000 to offset the tax due on her estate.

You need to look back the 7 years from the date of death to 30 June 2014 to capture any gifts made.

In this case the gifts to Miss B and Mr C are caught within the 7-year timeframe preceding the date of death.

Accordingly, the nil rate band available to offset IHT against the estate assets is £175,000 namely £325,000 – £100,000 (Miss B gift) – £50,000 (Mr C gift).

The gift to Ms D was made too far back in time to be brought into account.

Example

Say Mrs A's Will leaves her estate equally between her sister's children, Miss E, Miss F and Mr H and her net estate at the date of death is £400,000. The balance of the estate which is subject to IHT is £75,000 (£400,000 – £325,000 NRB) and the IHT thereon is £30,000 (£75,000 x 40%). Administration expenses are £10,000. This means that each beneficiary will receive £120,000 each (namely (£400,000 – £30,000 IHT – £10,000 expenses)/3).

However, when taking account of the gifts in the first example, the residue of the estate changes so that each beneficiary will receive £100,000. This is calculated by:

Net estate at date of death = £400,000

Available NRB to offset against estate at date of death = £325,000 – £100,000 Miss B gift – £50,000 Mr C gift = £175,000

Estate subject to IHT = £400,000 (net estate) – £175,000 (available NRB) = £225,000.

Tax due on estate = £225,000 (estate subject to IHT) x 40% = £90,000

Residuary estate = £400,000 (net estate) – £90,000 (IHT) – £10,000 (administration expenses) = £300,000

Each beneficiary receives £100,000 (residuary estate / 3)

As you will see, the failed PETs have significantly reduced the amounts the residuary beneficiaries will receive from the estate.

Exempt Gifts

These are gifts that are exempt from IHT. There are different categories of exempt gifts as follows:

- Transfers between spouses/civil partners – these are completely free of IHT regardless of whether the transfer is 1p or £100m. To take advantage of this exemption, the spouse/civil partner must live permanently in the UK and be legally married or in a civil partnership with the donor. If either of these conditions are not met, then any benefit derived by the spouse will be treated as if the spouse is a non-exempt beneficiary.

- Annual exemption – each person has a £3,000 annual exemption which they can use to make gifts which will be free of IHT. This can either be a single transaction up to £3,000 or can be comprised of a series of smaller transactions up to that value. It can also be used as a part exemption against larger gifts. If an annual allowance has not been utilised, it can be carried forward to the following year but the annual allowance for the tax year of gift must be utilised first before the carried forward allowance can be used. You can only carry forward one year's unused annual allowance.

Example

A makes a gift of £10,000 to their friend B. A has made no other gifts during the current tax year. The tax treatment of the £10,000 gift will be £3,000 being exempt under the annual allowance and the £7,000 being a PET which requires to be survived by the donor by 7 years to fall out with the donor's estate.

Example

A makes a gift of £10,000 to their friend B. A has made no other gifts during the current tax year. A also made no gifts during the immediately preceding tax year. The tax treatment of the £10,000 gift will be £3,000 being exempt under the current year's annual allowance, a further £3,000 being exempt under the previous year's annual allowance and the £4,000 balance being a PET which requires to be survived by the donor by 7 years to fall out with the donor's estate.

Small gifts

You can make any number of gifts to any number of individuals up to the total value of £250 per recipient in any tax year and it will be free of IHT. The condition is that the **total** of the gifts to any **one person** must **not** exceed £250 **in a single tax year**. If the total gift(s) to a person does exceed £250, then you need to look at whether the annual allowance will apply in full or in part to the gift to prevent the gift being subject to IHT. Any part of the gift not covered by a relief or exemption will be a PET.

Example

A makes the following gifts during tax year 2020/2021:

- B – £95
- C – £105 and £54
- D – £56 and £100
- E – £145

As the total of all gifts made by A to each beneficiary are under £250 within the relevant tax year, each gift falls within the small gifts exemption and are exempt from IHT.

Example

A makes the following gifts during tax year 2020/2021:

- B – £95
- C – £205 and £54
- D – £56 and £100
- E – £145 and £110

In this situation, only the gifts to B and D would fall within the small gifts exemption. The gifts to C and E do not qualify for the small gifts exemption as they total in excess of £250 to each beneficiary. In this case, the gifts to C and E will take up £259 and £255 respectively from A's annual allowance.

Gifts to UK charities

Gifts to UK charities are exempt from IHT. The charity must be registered within the UK to qualify. Foreign charities do not qualify for this exemption and gifts to foreign charities will be PETs or Failed PETs as the case may be.

Gifts to UK political parties[91]

These types of gifts are exempt from IHT although gifts to national parties over £7,500 must be declared publicly as must gifts over £1,500 to local associations. In order to qualify, the party being donated to must have had at the last election:

1. at least 2 MPs voted in; or

---

91 S24 IHTA 1984

2. One MP voted in with 150,000 votes[92].

If the party does not meet either criteria then the gift will be classed as a PET.

Gifts on marriage

The amount of a gift that will be exempt on marriage depends on the relationship of the recipient to the donor. Gifts of up to £5,000 in favour of a child will be exempt. This amount reduces to £2,500 where the recipient is a grandchild of the donor and reduces further to £1,000 to anyone else (including your fiancé/fiancée!). For this exemption to work, the gift must be given in contemplation of a specific marriage and the marriage must take place. It is not sufficient to give a gift in contemplation that the person may one day get married.

When is a PET not a PET?

Another trap for the unwary in identifying gifts is in situations where the deceased has given away an asset but still retains a benefit. This is known as a gift with reservation of benefit (GWR, GWRB or GWROB for short). In this situation, the 7-year PET clock does not start ticking until the donor ceases to have a benefit from the gift. The most common situation where you will come across this is where the deceased owned a property and then gifted it to one or more of their children during their lifetime but continued to live in the property. In this case, the value of the gift is the value of the asset at the time the deceased ceased to have a benefit from the asset rather than the value at the date of the gift.

Example

A owns a property worth £200,000. A gifts the property to their children B and C on 1 July 2007. A continues to reside in the property until their death on 31 December 2017. At the time of A's death, the property was

92 Banks V HMRC, 2018 UKFTT 617 TC

worth £250,000. The value of the gift brought back into account for the estate is £250,000.

Example

A owns a property worth £300,000. A gifts the property to their child B on 21 August 2003. A continues to reside in the property until A moved into permanent residential care death on 14 February 2016 at which point B moves into the property. A dies on 31 June 2019. At the time that A moved into permanent residential care the property was worth £390,000 and at the time of their death, the property was worth £425,000. The gift became a PET on 14 February 2016 as the deceased received no further benefit from the asset and the value attributable to the gift is £390,000

A GWROB can be avoided by the donor paying an open market rental for the use of the asset. This is known as a pre-owned asset tax or POAT for short. By paying for the use of the asset, it allows the usual 7-year clock to start ticking immediately to lift the asset out of your estate. The conditions to meet the pre-owned asset tax rules are that:

1. You must pay an open market rent for the use of the asset;

2. The asset needs to be valued every 5 years where the POAT charge is in place to ensure that a fair market rent continues to be paid;

3. Where a full market value rent is paid for the asset, the Inheritance Tax charge will not apply;

4. POAT is a charge to Income Tax rather than IHT despite its application in respect of the operation of gifts.

As you might imagine, clients are likely to be less than receptive to the suggestion that having acquired an asset and chosen to give away ownership that in order for it to leave their estate, they have to pay even more money out!

Chargeable Lifetime Transfer otherwise known as a CLT

This is a gift which unlike a PET is immediately subject to an IHT charge. This will occur where the donor makes a settlement into a relevant property trust (RPT) which when added together with all other CLTs made in the 7 years prior to this settlement exceed the nil rate band. Unlike regular gifts, the IHT charge is levied at the lifetime IHT rate of 20% rather than the estate rate of 40%. If the donor dies within 7 years of the CLT, a further 20% becomes chargeable on the gift bringing it up to the estate rate of 40%.

The backwards shadow

This is where the gifts in the 14 years prior to death rule comes in. It will apply where a PET fails in the 7 years prior to death. In that case, it is necessary to then look at the gifts that have been made in the 7 years prior to the PET that failed. Where there have been CLT's made in the 7 years prior to the failed PET, these will require to be taken into account when calculating the IHT due in connection with the estate.

Example

A settles £275,000 into a discretionary trust on 4 July 2008. A had not made any gifts of any description prior to this settlement. This is a CLT but as it is under the applicable NRB at the time of settlement, there is no IHT to pay on the settlement into the trust.

A then gifts cash to his god daughter B of £500,000 on 4 January 2014. This is a PET. There will be no IHT due on the occasion of this gift and will fall out with A's estate if A survives until 5 January 2021.

The CLT will only affect the PET if A fails to survive until 5 January 2021.

A dies on 14 February 2020. A's net estate at date of death is worth £400,000. The NRB at the time of A's death is £325,000.

The treatment of the CLT and the PET are as follows:

The CLT uses the first £275,000 of the NRB leaving £50,000 of the NRB available.

The next claim on the NRB is the now failed PET. £50,000 (being the remaining amount of the NRB) is deducted from the value of the PET leaving £450,000 of the failed PET chargeable to IHT at 40%. Taper Relief will apply to reduce the effective rate of IHT due on the failed PET as the failed PET was made between 3-7 years before A's death (see below for further information).

There is no NRB available to offset any IHT in the estate assets and therefore the full £400,000 of estate is subject to IHT at 40%.

Had A died on 30 July 2021, the PET would not have failed and would have been out with the 7 years of the date of death. As such, it would not be counted for IHT purposes. As the PET was successful, the CLT is also not brought back into account. As no other gifts were made by A before his death, the full NRB is available to offset the IHT due on the estate.

Taper Relief

Taper relief applies to failed PETs to reduce the amount of IHT payable where the collective PETs exceed the NRB applicable at the time of the death. Taper relief is payable on the balance of the collective PETs over the NRB. The effective rate of IHT that will apply to failed PETs is dependent on the length of time between the failed PET being made and the death of the donor. The applicable rates of IHT for failed PETs are as follows:

Period of years before death when gift was made	% reduction in IHT (Taper Relief)	IHT payable on gift above NRB
0-3 years	0%	40%
3-4 years	20%	32%
4-5 years	40%	24%
5-6 years	60%	16%
6-7 years	80%	8%
In excess of 7 years	N/A	N/A

Business Property Relief (BPR)

This is a relief which applies to reduce the IHT due on certain business assets. In order to qualify for the relief, the deceased must have held the asset upon which relief is sought for a minimum of two years prior to their death.

Once the time frame qualification has been met, the relief can apply at either 50% or 100%.

100% relief will operate on:

- A business or interest in a business; or
- Shares in an unlisted (privately owned) business

50% relief will operate on:

- A shareholding in a listed (publicly owned) company which controls more than 50% of the voting rights in the company

- Land, buildings and/or machinery owned by the deceased and which was used in a business in which they were a partner or otherwise controlled

- Land, buildings and/or machinery used in a business and which is held in a trust that the business has the right to benefit from

It is important to note that in respect of business interests, the business must be a fully trading business. A business which consists of activities that are wholly or mainly related to making investments will not qualify for the relief. A property investment business will (more than likely) be a business which is considered to be one which consists wholly or mainly of making investments and will not qualify for the relief. By comparison, a business which is a retail enterprise is likely on the face of it to qualify for the relief. A business such as a nursery which owns its own building is also likely to qualify for the relief for while it owns its own building, the majority to the activities within the business are trading activities and the ownership of the building is an incidental rather than a main trading activity. The key point to note is that each business will turn on its own facts as to whether it qualifies for the relief. There is a myriad of case law on this point which will be useful if you find yourself staring down the barrel of an argument with HMRC over whether the business is a trading business or one consisting of wholly or mainly making investments.

BPR can apply for gifts made within 7 years of the death of the original owner. In order to qualify for the relief, the recipient must have continued to hold the asset in a business context from the date of gift to the date of death (although certain property can be replaced such as machinery so long as it is of equal value and continues to be used in the business during the relevant period) and the deceased must have owned the asset for two years prior to making the gift.

Agricultural Property Relief (APR)

This is predominantly land used for farming purposes but also includes ancillary items such as farm houses and land subject to grazing leases.

This relief has a two or seven-year qualification period. The two-year period applies where the land is physically occupied by the owner, the owner's business or the owner's spouse or civil partner for agricultural purposes. The seven-year period applies where the land is occupied by someone else for agricultural purposes eg tenanted.

APR relief at 100% is available if:

- the person who owned the land farmed it themselves;
- the land was used by someone else on a short-term grazing licence;
- it was let on a tenancy that began on or after 1 September 1995;
- certain properties which were owned before 10 March 1981[93].

In all other cases, relief is restricted to 50%.

This should be, on the face of it, a straightforward relief – either you qualify or you don't. There is however a huge raft of case law on what can qualify under the legislation, a lot of which concerns the character of the farm house. Farm houses are likely to be the major source of angst for you as to whether they will qualify for the relief. In short, they must be occupied by the deceased, a farm employee or certain connected relations and must be of a nature and size appropriate to farming activities so large farm houses on a small farm are going to cause (and have caused if the case law is anything to go by!) difficulties.

You cannot claim both BPR and APR on an asset and therefore as BPR is (usually) the relief that will provide the highest amount of relief, in

93 For further information see https://www.gov.uk/guidance/agricultural-relief-on-inheritance-tax#rates-of-agricultural-relief

circumstances where both reliefs would apply, you would normally elect to claim BPR rather than APR.

2024 Autumn Budget changes to APR and BPR

Following the budget in October 2024, changes are expected to come into force in relation to both BPR and APR. While at the time of writing this book, we have yet to have sight of a Finance Bill, it is anticipated that the following changes to APR and BPR will occur from 6 April 2026:

1. 100% relief will be available for both BPR and APR up to a combined allowance of £1m;

2. For claims over the £1m allowance, APR and BPR will be reduced to 50% relief;

3. The combined allowance will include claims made on death, failed potentially exempt transfers and chargeable lifetime transfers;

4. Anti forestalling provisions have been included which means that the new rules will apply to failed PETS made on or after 30 October 2024 where the death occurs on or after 6 April 2026;

5. BPR will be reduced to 50% for investments not listed on a recognised stock exchange. A full list of recognised stock exchanges for these purposes can be found at https://www.gov.uk/government/publications/designated-recognised-stock-exchanges-section-1005-income-tax-act-2007/designated-recognised-stock-exchanges-section-1005-income-tax-act-2007-v3. This will therefore affect portfolio planning using the Alternative Investment Market (AIM) which is used by some tax and investment planners as a relatively quick solution to put assets outwith a person's estate for IHT purposes with the holdings only currently being required to be held for 2 years to qualify for 100% relief. It is anticipated that this relief

will not be affected by the £1m allowance mentioned above and therefore BPR portfolios of shares are likely to still retain at least some of their attractiveness for IHT planning (warning – always consult a financial adviser before looking at investing in this type of investment as it is not suitable for everyone with an IHT problem); and

6. It is not anticipated that the combined allowance will be transferable to a spouse on death unlike the current nil rate band or residential enhancement to the nil rate band.

From 6 April 2025, it is anticipated that the application of APR will be extended to include land managed under an environmental agreement with, or on behalf of, the UK government, devolved governments, public bodies, local authorities, or relevant approved responsible bodies.

In short, when dealing with APR and BPR, check if legislation has been introduced since 30 October 2024 which affects your particular case.

<u>Grossing</u>

Where there is no direction as to who should pay the IHT on legacies, the IHT due will be born by the legatee.

<u>Example</u>

A dies with a net estate worth £1.2m. A leaves a gift to their friend B of £400,000 and the residue to A's spouse, C. No gifts were made in the 7 years before A's death. The tax on £400,000 would be £400,000 – (£400,000-£325,000 = £75,000 x 40%) = £30,000. B therefore receives £370,000 (£400,000-£30,000) and C receives £800,000.

However, where the legacy is left free of IHT, this means that the legatee will need to receive the amount stated in the Will rather than the amount stated less the IHT due. The effect of this is that the exempt beneficiaries will receive less from the estate than they otherwise would have done had the legacy been subject to IHT. A calculation has to be done to gross up the legacy to take account of the IHT due.

Example

A dies with a net estate worth £1.2m. A leaves a gift to their friend B of £400,000 free of IHT and the residue to A's spouse, C. No gifts were made in the 7 years before A's death. B's legacy is calculated as follows:

Legacy per Will	£400,000
LESS: NRB	£325,000
Taxable element	£ 75,000
£75,000 x (100/60) =	£125,000 + £325,000 (NRB) = £450,000 = grossed up legacy

C will receive £750,000 as residue which is £50,000 less than C would have received had B's legacy been subject to IHT rather than net of IHT.

You can cross check this calculation (and when it comes to IHT, cross checking is always essential as the tax has the propensity to fry even the most spectacular of tax brains!) by checking the amount of tax due on the grossed up legacy and deducting it from the grossed up legacy. The answer should equal the legacy per the Will.

Example

Per the above example, £450,000-£325,000 (NRB) = £125,000 x 40% = £50,000 IHT due. £450,000-£50,000 IHT due = £400,000 which equals the legacy.

Reclaiming Inheritance Tax

If Inheritance Tax has been overpaid, it can be reclaimed from HMRC. HMRC will repay any overpaid Inheritance Tax with interest at the Bank of England base rate minus 1 percentage point, subject to a minimum interest rate of 0.5%.

Executors may overpay Inheritance Tax for a variety of reasons, such as having lodged an IHT400 with estimated values which are later confirmed to have been overstated, overpayment has been made in case any estimated values have been understated or because assets were originally thought to have belonged to the estate but on making a claim for realisation, the Executors discover they were written in trust.

It is also possible to reclaim inheritance tax paid on certain assets that are sold at a loss within a certain time frame after death. This can be done in respect of the following assets:

1. Stocks and shares

2. Land and buildings

To reclaim IHT paid on stocks and shares, you need to complete Form IHT35[94].

In order to reclaim the tax on stocks and shares, the following criteria must apply:

1. Only qualifying investments sold by the Executors within 12 months of date of death can qualify for a refund. Any shares transferred to a beneficiary from the estate who subsequently decides to sell the shares does not qualify for the relief;

2. The refund is calculated on the net loss incurred across the total value of all shares sold – not just the ones sold at a loss;

94 https://www.gov.uk/government/publications/inheritance-tax-claim-for-relief-loss-on-sale-of-shares-iht35

3. The effective date for the sale of the investments is the contracted date, not the date when sale proceeds are received; and

4. The IHT35 needs to be submitted within 4 years of the date of death.

Qualifying investments for these purposes are:

1. Shares and securities that were listed on a recognised stock exchange at the date of death;

2. UK Government stock (gilts); and

3. Holdings in unit trusts;

To reclaim IHT paid on land and buildings, you need to complete Form IHT38[95].

1. To qualify for the relief:

2. the land and buildings must be sold at a loss from the date of death value within 4 years of the date of death (or 3 years for deaths on or before 15 March 1990);

3. The relief is restricted if any properties have been purchased in the 4-year time frame;

4. There must be an overall net loss of £1,000 or 5% of the value of the land on date of death, whichever is lower;

5. The effective date for the sales is the date of conclusion of missives; and

---

95 https://www.gov.uk/government/publications/inheritance-tax-claim-for-relief-loss-on-sale-of-land-iht38

6. Relief is normally disallowed whereby the purchaser is a beneficiary or a relative of a beneficiary

Adjustments to Inheritance Tax

If you need to adjust the inheritance tax value of an asset, for example, because an asset holder has provided you with an incorrect date of death value, this can be done by:

1. letter to HMRC[96] where there are only one or two adjustments; or

2. on form C4[97] where there are a significant number of adjustments to be made but you do not need to confirm to the asset; or

3. On Form C4(S) where in addition to intimating a change of value, you require to obtain Confirmation to one or more of the affected assets (Eik).

Where the net figure has increased as a consequence of the adjustments, you will need to pay any additional inheritance tax that falls due along with any interest.

96 Inheritance Tax, HM Revenue and Customs, BX9 1HT

97 https://www.gov.uk/government/publications/inheritance-tax-corrective-account-c4

CHAPTER SEVENTEEN

INCOME TAX

Income tax will apply up to the date of the deceased's death and also for the period of administration of the estate.

Date of Death Income Tax

You will need to finalise the deceased's Income Tax position to date of death. To this end, when undertaking the initial investigations into the extent of the estate, you should ask for details of the income and the tax deducted (if any) from the assets for the tax year in which the deceased died and the preceding tax year. You should also ask HMRC for a copy of the deceased's last tax return (if they filed one).

If the deceased had an accountant, the Executors can employ the accountant to bring all matters up to date. The accountants' expenses will be a legitimate expense of the administration of the estate. In any event, you will need to provide the accountant with details of the relevant income.

Where there is no accountant or where the deceased did not have to complete a self-assessment tax return (SA100) (for example, where all tax was deducted at source), then you will need to make sure that the deceased has paid the right amount of tax to date of death. Where the deceased has paid too much tax, a refund will be due to the estate.

It used to be the case that you would fill in a short form tax return for a deceased person which would confirm the tax due to or by the estate. Some years ago, HMRC did away with this procedure and work out the tax due to or by the estate from the information they have received from asset holders through real time reporting. However, the fatal flaw in this particular plan is that it does not take account of chargeable events which can affect the amount of Income Tax due on an estate.

What is a chargeable event?

A chargeable event can occur when money is taken out of an investment bond. An investment bond is generally a single premium whole of life policy which has an investment value which can rise and fall like any other stock market related product. While the chargeable event is triggered by a gain arising on liquidation, the tax charge that applies is Income Tax rather than Capital Gains Tax[98]. A chargeable event can be triggered by the following types of events;

1. Death of the policy holder where the death gives rise to a benefit;
2. Assignment of all rights under the policy for money or money's worth;
3. Maturity of the investment bond;
4. Partial surrender or assignments;
5. Policy loans;
6. Surrender of all rights under the policy; or
7. Reclassification of the bond as a personal portfolio bond;

Death of the policy holder will only trigger a chargeable event where the death triggers a benefit e.g. the bond comes to an end on the death. If a bond is taken out on a joint life, second death basis, there will be no chargeable event on the first death as the bond does not end on the first

[98] S461 (1) Income Tax (Trading and Other Income) Act (ITTOIA) 2005

death but there will be a chargeable event on the second death as the bond will terminate at that time.

It is important to understand the reasons which will trigger a chargeable event to avoid a chargeable event arising unnecessarily during the administration of the estate when you go to realise the bond.

A gift of a bond will not trigger a chargeable event unless cash or assets are exchanged. It is therefore possible to assign out some or all of the bond to non or lower rate tax payers without triggering a chargeable event. The beneficiary can thereafter encash their share of the bond which may trigger a chargeable event which will be payable at that beneficiary's marginal rate of tax. This means that you can effectively manage the amount of tax which will be paid and avoid triggering excess tax to be paid within the estate. This of course depends on the terms of the Will or Intestacy as to whether there is any flexibility to order matters in a tax efficient way. You may be stuck with the rules of the Will/intestacy and have no discretion over who gets what and when.

Partial surrenders can also trigger a chargeable event. Under the bond rules, you can withdraw up to 5% of the original capital settled into the bond per policy year without triggering an immediate charge to tax. If you were to do this annually, it would take 20 years to exhaust the original capital. You will frequently come across this being referred to by clients as them receiving an income from the bond. It is not in fact income as such but a return of a specified amount of capital. The withdrawal is however assessed for Income tax purposes if you withdraw more than 5% of the capital in a single year. It is however possible to carry forward any unused allowances. Any withdrawals over and above the annual 5% plus any carry forward unused allowances will trigger a chargeable event.

Example

A settled £100,000 into an investment bond on 1 January 2017.

A draws down £9,000 on 30 July 2018.

A can drawdown £5,000 per policy year without triggering an immediate charge to tax (5% of the £100,000 initial capital).

As no drawdowns were made in the first year, the first year's unused £5,000 carries forward to the second year giving a total available drawdown of £10,000 in that year without triggering a chargeable event.

As the £9,000 drawn down is less than the available £10,000, no chargeable event occurs on the draw down.

A then wishes to draw down a further £9,000 on 25 September 2019. The total available allowance before triggering a chargeable event will be £5,000 (year 1) + £5,000 (year 2) + £5,000 (year 3) – £9,000 (year 2) = £6,000. If A draws down the £9,000 in 2019, there will be a gain and therefore a chargeable event of £3,000 (£9,000 – £6,000) on the draw down. This can be avoided if A takes £6,000 or less from the bond on 25 September 2019.

If at 1st January 2019, A invested a further £200,000 into the bond, the available allowance for the 25 September 2019 drawdown would be as follows:

Year 1 (1 January 2017 – 31 December 2017) = £5,000 (5% of Settlement 1 of £100,000)

Year 2 (1 January 2018 – 31 December 2018) = £5,000 (5% of Settlement 1 of £100,000)

Year 3 (1 January 2019 – 31 December 2019) = £15,000 (5% of Settlement 1 of £100,000 + 5% of Settlement 2 of £200,00)

Total available to drawdown between years 1 – 3 – £25,000 (Year 1 £5,000 + Year 2 £5,000 + Year 3 – £15,000)

Less

Withdrawal Year 2 (1 January 2018 – 31 December 2018) = £9,000 (Settlement 1)

Equals

Available allowance of £16,000.

As the available allowance of £16,000 exceeds the second proposed draw down of £9,000 in year 3, the second £9,000 could be drawn down from a mix of both bonds without triggering a chargeable event.

A dies on 30 January 2021. As it was a single life assured bond, the bond comes to an end, and a chargeable event will arise on the termination.

If it had been a joint life, second death bond between A & B, there would be no chargeable event arising on A's death and the bond would continue until the earlier of encashment or B's death.

Income Tax for the period of administration

You will also need to ensure that all Income Tax is accounted for during the period of administration of the estate.

Do I need to make a declaration to HMRC?

Short answer? Maybe.

For deaths up to 5 April 2024, where the estate received bank account interest only that did not exceed £500, there was/is no requirement to report the income from the period of administration to HMRC and to account for tax which would otherwise fall due.

For deaths on or after 6 April 2024, the restriction on the qualifying type of income for the non-reporting exemption was lifted and now includes all income arising within the period of administration as long as it does not exceed £500. **Do not** include ISA income (more of which later) which has arisen in years 1–3 of the administration of the estate when calculating whether your income for the relevant period is under or over the £500 de minimis level.

Where income during the period of administration exceeds £500, tax will be payable on the full amount and you will need to report the income and liability to HMRC. You should note that in calculating the tax due on the estate, estates do not have a personal allowance so all income is immediately subject to the applicable category of tax.

Reporting income tax to HMRC can be done in one of two ways:

1. Informal method; or

2. Formal method

Informal Method

This can be done informally with HMRC through a letter, production of your Income Tax calculation along with a cheque for the tax you have calculated to be due where the following conditions apply:

1. The estate at date of death was worth less than £2.5m;

2. Estate realised in the tax year that you are dealing with is £500,000 or less; and

3. The total Income Tax and Capital Gains Tax for the tax year you are dealing with is less than £10,000

Formal Method

Where one or more of these conditions is not met, you will need to submit a formal tax return (SA900). As with the tax to date of death, you may wish to employ an accountant to do this for you. If you do not have an accountant employed in the estate, you will need to register the estate for Income Tax before you can submit the tax return at https://www.gov.uk/guidance/register-your-clients-estate You will need an agent services account to be able to register your client's estate. If you do not have one, you can create one the first time that you go to register an estate. Bear in mind that if you need to obtain an agent services account log in id, you will need a couple of weeks for the log in details to be received so make sure you leave enough time to obtain one against the deadlines for registration.

The deadline for registering an estate with HMRC is 5 October in the tax year after the tax year that you require to submit the tax return for.

Alternatively, you can ask the Executors to register the estate themselves.

Example

If you require to declare underpaid tax for the tax year 2020/2021 then you will need to register the estate by 5 October 2021.

Once your estate is registered with HMRC, HMRC will issue a unique tax payer reference (UTR) for the estate which will need to be quoted on the tax return.

Tax Rate

Estates are taxed at the basic rate of tax as applied by the Westminster Government. The Scottish Rate of Income Tax (SRIT) does not apply to estates.

ISA

ISA income is taxed differently to the rest of the estate income. As with the position before death, for the first 3 years post death, any income and gains remain tax free within the estate.

R185e

Where income arises in an estate, you will need to notify the residuary beneficiaries of their share of the income and the tax paid thereon as they will need to report the income on their tax return. Where the beneficiary is a higher rate tax payer, they will need to pay the difference between the tax paid by the estate and the tax due as a higher rate tax payer. Likewise where the beneficiary is a non or lower rate tax payer, they can reclaim the tax paid by the estate on their behalf. The income is reported annually by the Executors using form R185e[99].

In order to calculate the income and tax that needs to be reported on the R185e, you will need to know the following:

1. The amount paid to the beneficiary from the estate in the tax year in question;

2. The share or shares of the net income due to the beneficiary in each tax rated category (for these purposes, this is the share of the income less tax due and either paid at source or paid through the estate). There are 3 categories of income tax in the period of administration:

    a. 0% or tax-free income – This would include ISA income arising within the first 3 years of the administration of an estate.

[99] https://assets.publishing.service.gov.uk/government/uploads/system/uploads/attachment_data/file/603950/R185_Estate_Income__03_17.pdf

b. 8.75% – this is the rate applicable to dividends arising on or after 6 April 2022. Prior to that, the rate applicable was 7.5%. The notional 10% dividend tax rate of 10% was abolished from 6 April 2016.

c. 20% – all other income (including ISA income arising in years 4 onwards of the administration of an estate)

If the amount paid to the beneficiary in the relevant tax year equals their share of the net income or exceeds it, the full amount of their share of the income and tax paid is allocated to them on the R185e. If however the payment to the beneficiary in the tax year is less than the net income allocated to them, it is only the sum equal to the amount they have received that is credited on the R185e along with the tax paid. Any balance of income/tax paid thereon is put in reserve and carried forward to the next tax year of the administration of the estate (if there is one).

Example

A is entitled to a 50% share of the residue in the estate of the late Joe Bloggs.

A receives an interim payment of residue from the estate during tax year 2023/2024. In the same year, income arises of £200 in the estate with a deduction of £40 made at the 20% tax rate. A is entitled to £100 of that income and credit of £20 tax (being one half share of both income and tax paid).

If A's interim payment from the estate during the tax year totalled £500, the full £100 income and tax due of £20 would be attributed to them in the R185e.

If, however, A's interim payment from the estate during the tax year totalled only £50, £50 of income and tax due of £10 would be attributed to them in the R185e. The remaining £50 with £10 tax paid would be carried forward to the next year and allocated against any further payments being made to that beneficiary from the estate in that tax year.

CHAPTER EIGHTEEN

CAPITAL GAINS TAX

Capital Gains Tax (CGT) does apply to estates but not in the same way as it does to individuals. You therefore need to check whether any disposal of an asset during the administration of the estate triggers a gain that needs to be reported.

If you are not confident in calculating the CGT that may be due in the estate, you should outsource to either the deceased's accountant (if they had one) or a reputable accountant whom you have encountered through your networking. You may also have an inhouse tax department who can assist you with the tax calculation.

Your principal goal here should be to identify if you have a tax problem and what steps need to be taken to identify the same and make payment – not necessarily that you should become a whizz at CGT. The last thing you need is for tax issue to arise post wind up and distribution of the estate whereby the Executor will be personally liable for settling the CGT liability and will thereafter be looking towards your indemnity policy for restitution if this is something which should have been within your foresight to deal with.

When does CGT arise?

CGT will be triggered when an asset is sold at a gain from its acquisition cost. For estates, the acquisition cost of an asset is uplifted to the date of death value, regardless of when it was originally purchased by the deceased and the price paid[100]. It is therefore important that you keep this in mind when getting assets valued at date of death as the value attributed to the asset not only determines the Inheritance Tax that is

[100] S62(1) Taxation of Capital Gains Act 1992

due on the estate but also the base cost for establishing any subsequent gains and losses on the estate.

If your estate crosses several tax years, it is sensible to keep a record of what assets are sold in each tax year to calculate whether CGT will become payable.

Annual allowance

The annual allowance which applies to an estate is the same as the annual allowance which applies to individuals which at the time of writing this book was £3,000[101]. You can check current and historic annual allowances at https://www.gov.uk/guidance/capital-gains-tax-rates-and-allowances#tax-free-allowances-for-capital-gains-tax The CGT annual allowance is a use it or lose it relief – if it is not utilised during the applicable tax year, it cannot be carried forward to the next year allow though losses can be.

There is however one very important difference between CGT for estates and individuals and that is the length of time that an annual allowance will apply to estates. Individuals annual allowance renews every year for the lifetime of the individual. For estates, Executors only have an annual allowance for the three years following the death[102]. Thereafter no annual allowance applies to any disposals of assets. The effect of this is that if assets continue to be held in the estate following the expiry of the three tax years, there will be no annual allowance to offset any gains made. It is therefore in everyone's interests to realise assets as far as possible within the first three tax years to take advantage of the annual allowance to minimise the tax that needs to be paid by the estate.

[101] November 2024

[102] S62(2) Taxation of Capital Gains Act 1992

The three years allowance runs from the date of death. Depending on where the deceased died in the tax year, the first year's allowance may not be capable of being utilised.

<u>Example</u>

Mr A dies on 3 March 2020. The tax years that will carry the Executors annual allowance are:

1. 2020/2021
2. 2021/2022
3. 2022/2023

As you will only have 33 days of the 2020/2021 tax year left following the death, it is unlikely that your Executors will be in a position to utilise the allowance and it is essentially lost. The net effect of this is that practically speaking, the Executor only has two years annual allowance to use.

<u>Example</u>

Mr B dies on 6 April 2020. The tax years that will carry the Executors annual allowance are:

1. 2020/2021
2. 2021/2022
3. 2022/2023

Compared to foregoing example, the Executor will have almost 3 full years to administer the estate and take advantage of all three years allowances.

TIP – where your deceased dies close to the expiry of the tax year and if, based on your initial meeting and assessment of the paperwork presented, the estate is likely to be of such a magnitude that it is likely to be subject to Inheritance Tax and it contains a portfolio of shares, you may wish to consider whether you ought to have the Executors instruct the broker to sell down a sufficient part of the portfolio to utilise the CGT allowance for the tax year of the date of death. Most discretionary fund manager (DFM) houses will allow you to do so ahead of Confirmation being granted where the ultimate recipient of the funds is going to be HMRC. This is trickier where the deceased's portfolio of shares are held in certificated form or in electronic format with individual Registrars as they will frequently insist on sight of Confirmation before executing any sales. The DFM will normally require an undertaking from the Executors to put the DFM back into the position they would have been in had they not acted on the instruction – for example, where a competing Executor arises or ultimately it is found that your Executor does not have the title to authorise the sale. Depending on the extent of the Inheritance Tax due, you may not need to utilise the whole allowance to raise the funds from the portfolio but you should certainly consider whether you should do so to take advantage of all allowances particularly if the death occurs at a time of rising markets where the portfolio may be subject to a gain even a short time after the death. Needless to say, the DFM's will not usually release the funds to HMRC until they have also had sight of a copy of the IHT400.

Deductible Allowances

Aside from the annual allowance, it is also possible to reduce the gain due on an estate by deducting certain allowances, for example, the costs of sale. All of the available allowances that can apply to the estate are outwith the remit of this book but for further information, I would commend to you Tolleys on Capital Gains Tax year book[103] which is updated

[103] https://www.lexisnexis.co.uk/store/products/tolley-s-capital-gains-tax-2024-25.html

annually. Suffice it to say, if you have a particularly complicated transaction such as the sale of farmland which is being sold to developers and for which may take several years to negotiate a sale and incur a myriad of expenses in the interim, employ an accountant to ensure that the estate does not pay more tax than it should.

Rates of CGT

The rate of CGT that will apply to each transaction will depend on the asset being sold. The applicable rates of CGT for Executors at the time of writing this book[104] is 24% (from 30 October 2024 to 5 April 2025). From 6 April 2025, the applicable rates will be:

1. 24% for property gains

2. 20% for all other gains

The rates do change from time to time (most recently in the October 2024 budget) so ensure you check the applicable rates for the relevant tax year on HMRC's website[105].

Please note that this is different to the rates which apply to individuals in life.

How to report CGT

You can use the informal method to report CGT to HMRC where **all** of the following circumstances apply:

1. The value of the estate at date of death was less than £2.5m;

---

[104] November 2024

[105] https://www.gov.uk/guidance/capital-gains-tax-rates-and-allowances

2. The total Income Tax and Capital Gains Tax for the applicable tax year totals less than £10,000; and

3. The total amount of assets realised within the current tax year does not exceed £500,000

The informal method is simply to write to HMRC with the name of the deceased, their national insurance number, a copy of your calculation, a statement in your covering letter which confirms that all of the above conditions apply, a request to deal with the tax position for the administration of the estate to be dealt with under the informal method and a cheque for the tax due. If the estate concluded within the tax year you are writing to HMRC about, you should also confirm that in your letter with a request to close off the estate's records. HMRC will normally write back to confirm acceptance of the position or they will raise queries.

In the event that your estate does not meet all of the above conditions, it will be necessary for you to register the estate for self-assessment. This is now done online via https://www.gov.uk/guidance/register-your-clients-estate

The estate must be registered online by the 5 October after the tax year when the estate starts to receive income or has chargeable gains on which tax is payable. HMRC will thereafter issue the estate with a Unique Taxpayer Reference (also known as an UTR) which will used to file the tax return.

In order to register the estate, you will need the following information to register the estate:

- The deceased's name

- The deceased's last known address

- The deceased's date of birth

- The deceased's date of death
- The deceased's National Insurance number (if available)
- The name of the estate, for example, "The estate of Joseph Bloggs, deceased"
- An address for the estate and contact telephone number (this will usually be the lead Executor's address and number)
- The Executor's name
- The Executor's address
- The Executor's date of birth
- The Executor's national insurance number (or passport number with expiry date)
- The Executor's telephone number and an email address
- If applicable, the date the administration period ended.

You can file a paper return up to 31 October in the tax year following the tax year in which the gain was triggered or you have until 31 January of the next year to file the return online. You will need an agent services account if you want to file online. This can be created at https://www.access.service.gov.uk/login/signin/creds.

All tax due will in any event be payable by 31 January of the year following the tax year that you are reporting on.

Selling land & buildings

If you are selling a property within an estate that gives rise to a gain, there is an additional procedure in addition to the above. The Executors are required to pay the CGT due on the sale of the property within 60 days of completion of the sale[106] – regardless of whether other sales of assets in the estate would give rise to an overall loss in the applicable year. This can either be done online[107] or you can request a form directly from HMRC[108]. Upon submission, HMRC will provide a specific reference number starting with an X to enable the tax to be paid. A reclaim of overpaid tax when taking into account other disposals undertaken in the same year as the sale of the property will need to be undertaken in the overall self-assessment tax return.

---

106 For sales that took place on or after 27 October 2021.

107 https://www.gov.uk/report-and-pay-your-capital-gains-tax/if-you-sold-a-property-in-the-uk-on-or-after-6-april-2020

108 https://www.gov.uk/government/organisations/hm-revenue-customs/contact/capital-gains-tax-enquiries-for-individuals-employees-and-self-employed

CHAPTER NINETEEN

BUSINESS DEVELOPMENT OPPORTUNITIES

The administration of the estate does not need to be the end of the business. There are a number of additional services which can be offered by your practice which can enhance the income generating opportunities from having an enhanced private client practice.

Deeds of Variation

As you circulate the schedule of assets during the administration of the estate prior to Confirmation, it is useful to raise the possibility of granting a Deed of Variation as often beneficiaries do not appreciate that they can vary their entitlement. This can then lead to a conversation regarding inheritance tax planning, succession planning, Wills and protecting assets against incapacity which then introduces the beneficiary as a new client to your firm.

Will review

You can also offer to review beneficiaries Wills during the administration of the estate to ensure that it continues to fit with the person's financial and family circumstances in light of their inheritance. Alternatively, you can offer to write a Will should they not have one. It is useful to offer this service prior to distributions being made as often clients are more likely to take advantage of this service where they do not physically have to pay you any money from their own pocket and the fees can be deducted from their share of the estate.

Power of Attorney

As with Wills, it is worthwhile asking about Powers of Attorney. As any good private client practitioner recognises, Powers of Attorney should be part of an individual's overall wealth management strategy. All too often, clients only come to us when mum has been diagnosed with dementia or otherwise where incapacity has already struck in which case it's a swift hand over to your litigation team to apply for guardianship. A power of attorney is not just for the elderly and should be marketed accordingly.

Conveyancing

Where a conveyancing transaction is being undertaken, it is always worthwhile asking the question of the person has a Will or Power of Attorney. If not, there is an opportunity for you to put one in place. Where there are existing documents in place, it is also an opportunity for you to review them to make sure that they still fit with the person's financial and family circumstances. The only thing worse than having no Will is having a Will which is outdated and which lands assets with entirely the wrong people.

Cohabiting couples

If you (or your colleagues) are acting in the purchase of a property involving a cohabiting couple, recommend that they put a Will in place which at least covers what happens to the house in the event of the death of one of them. The last thing a person needs on the death of their partner is to discover they are co-owners with an in-law:

1. They don't get on with;

2. Who insists on being bought out of the property which could bring financial hardship to the surviving partner;

3. Who forces a sale of the property where the cohabiting partner can't buy them out so the surviving partner loses both their house and their partner; or

4. Who insists on moving in beside the partner!

Likewise, it is always worth recommending that a cohabitation agreement is put in place when the couple are buying a house (or indeed moving in together in general). While no one hopes that a relationship will end, having a cohabitation agreement in place can at least make the financial aspects of the separation straight forward leaving "only" the emotional fall out to be dealt with. This is particularly important where one party is bringing more in wealth to the relationship then the other for example, the deposit from a sale of their previous property or a contribution from the Bank of Mum and Dad. This will ensure that the person bringing the additional funds does not lose out in the event of the need for a subsequent sale or transfer on separation. In this case, one person will need to have the ability to access independent financial and legal advice as the document will have been drafted by the solicitor acting for one party but if the other person has insufficient funds to take that advice, this can be covered by the instructing person in the agreement by way of an agreed contribution towards their partner's costs, say £250-300 plus VAT.

Push back on cohabitation agreements is usually the costs. The counter argument to that is that spending a few hundred pounds now will be far less than it will cost to reach a financial settlement in the event of a separation further down the line[109].

---

[109] See Law Society of Scotland conflicts guidance on preparing cohabitation agreements where your firm is acting in respect of a property purchase for the cohabiting couple – https://www.lawscot.org.uk/members/rules-and-guidance/rules-and-guidance/section-b/rule-b2/guidance/b2-1-pre-nuptial-cohabitation-and-separation-agreements/

Immigration Law

Particularly in these post-Brexit times, it is important to check the residence status of spouses/civil partners, cohabiting partners and children. Where it is found that someone is not a British National and their right to live in the UK was dependant on their relationship with the deceased, that person may have to apply for a new visa and they may require help in navigating the visa system. There are also different rules which will apply where the deceased died as a member of the armed forces.

Further information can be found at https://www.gov.uk/contact-ukvi-inside-outside-uk

Financial Advice

Beneficiaries of estates can inherit significant amounts of money. It is always worthwhile suggesting that they take independent financial advice. You may wish to make contact with a number of financial advisers who you can use for this type of business. That way, if your client wishes to take financial advice and they do not have an existing adviser, you can provide details of the various financial advisers that you work with and suggest to the client that they call round the advisers so that they can decide if they wish to take financial advice and which adviser they feel most comfortable with. Be sure to check whether the financial adviser is an independent or tied adviser and confirm with the beneficiary accordingly. Tied advisers will be restricted to the products of one or more investment companies. An independent financial adviser will be able to select the best products for the client from all of the available products and investment companies on the market. In turn, you may find that the financial advisers will start to introduce new clients to you.

CHAPTER TWENTY

USEFUL ADDRESSES AND CONTACT DETAILS

(CORRECT AS AT FEBRUARY 2025)

Banks

Bank of Scotland, Lloyds Bank, Halifax and MBNA
https://www.bankofscotland.co.uk/helpcentre/bereavement.html

Royal Bank of Scotland
https://www.rbs.co.uk/life-moments/bereavement.html#notify

TSB
https://www.tsb.co.uk/help-and-support/bereavement-and-coping-with-loss/#letting-us-know

Santander
https://bereavement-online.santander.co.uk/bereavement-frontend/index

Barclays
https://www.barclays.co.uk/what-to-do-when-someone-dies/notify-us/

Company Registrars

Equiniti
https://www.shareview.co.uk/4/Info/Portfolio/default/en/home/shareholders/BereavementSupport/Pages/Bereavement-Support.aspx

Computershare Investor Services PLC
The Pavilions
Bridgwater Road
Bristol
BS99 6ZZ

Link Asset Services
https://ww2.linkassetservices.com/bereavement/

Genealogists

Estate Research
102 Chapel Lane
Wigan
WN3 4HG
DX: 19316 Wigan
E: info@estateresearch.co.uk
T: 01942 826500

Fraser and Fraser
39 Hatton Garden
London
EC1N 8EH
DX: 53304 Clerkenwell
E: info@fraserandfraser.co.uk
T: +44 (0) 20 7832 1400
F: +44 (0) 20 7832 1450

Finders International
83 Princes Street
Edinburgh
EH2 2ER
E:
contact@findersinternational.co.uk
T: +44 (0) 131 278 0552
F: +44 (0)131 278 0548

Title Research
Spectrum House
Bond Street
Bristol
BS1 3LG
E: info@titleresearch.com
T: +44 (0) 345 87 27 600
F: +44 (0) 117 981 1474

Government Agencies

HMRC
Inheritance Tax
HM Revenue and Customs
BX9 1HT
T: 0300 123 1072

Department for Work and Pensions

To confirm if there are sums due to or by the estate:

Debt Management (RES)
Mail Handling Site A
Wolverhampton
WV98 2DH

For information relating to state benefits claimed by the deceased including tax information:

The Pension Service
Post Handling Site A
Wolverhampton
WV98 1AF

DVLA
https://www.gov.uk/tell-dvla-about-bereavement

Passport Office
https://www.gov.uk/government/publications/what-to-do-with-a-passport-when-the-passport-holder-has-died

Kings and Lord Treasurer's Remembrancer
https://www.kltr.gov.uk/content/contact-us
E: enquiries@kltr.gov.uk

The National Ultimus Haeres Unit
Procurator Fiscal Office
Cameronian House
3/5 Almada Street
Hamilton
ML3 0HG
E: NationalUltimusHaeresUnit@copfs.gov.uk
T: 0300 0204196 / 0141 420 8804

Bonds of Caution

Savendale
Hudson House
8 Albany Street
Edinburgh
EH1 2QB
T: 0131 473 1048
E: info@savendale.co.uk
W: www.savendale.co.uk

RSA
Bonds
3rd Floor
191 West George Street
Glasgow
G2 2LD
E: bonds@uk.rsagroup.com
T: 0141 285 8248
W: https://www.rsainsurance.co.uk/commercial-insurance-products/scottish-executry-bonds

The Central Chancery of the Orders of Knighthood

St James Palace
Marlborough Road
London
SW1A 1BS

CHAPTER TWENTY-ONE

FURTHER READING

This is by no means an exclusive list as there are many texts out there concerning the laws of succession in Scotland. The following reflects my view on the basics that you should either have in your private client library or otherwise have access to from your local law library if you are wanting to build an estates practice within your firm. These books will in turn lead you on elsewhere:

<u>**Succession Law**</u>

- "Bartos and Meston on the Succession (Scotland) Act 1964", W Green

- "Meston's Succession Opinions", W Green, 2000

- "A Practical Guide to Legal Rights in Scotland", Macdonald, S J, Law Brief Publishing

<u>**Cross jurisdictional estates**</u>

- "Anton on Private International Law", 3rd Edition, W Green

<u>**Court process and drafting Confirmation applications**</u>

- "Currie on Confirmation of Executors", 9th Edition, Scobbie, Eilidh M, W Green

- "Contentious Executries: Commissary and Executry Litigation in Scotland" Macleod, R A S, 2nd Edition, W Green

Drafting of Wills and interpretation

- "Drafting Wills in Scotland", Barr, Biggar, Dalgleish & Stevens, 2nd Edition, Bloomsbury Press
- "Drafting for Succession in Scotland", Kerrigan, J, 2nd Edition, W Green
- "Drafting Trusts and Will Trusts in Scotland; a Modern Approach", Kessler, J & Grant, W, 2nd Edition, W. Green

Tax

- "McCutcheon on Inheritance Tax", 7th Edition, Sweet & Maxwell as supplemented
- "Mellows Taxation for Executors and Trustees" LexisNexis (please note this publication is a loose-leaf subscription service publication which is updated three times per year so check you have the most up to date version)

Each of the following books published by Tolley/Lexis-Nexis referred to below are produced annually to take account of updates to law and practice. You should therefore check you have the correct year for the administration year in question.

- Tolley's Inheritance Tax
- Tolley's Income Tax
- Tolley's Capital Gains Tax
- Tolley's Tax Guide (short blast guide to various taxes)
- Whillans Tax Tables

Journals

- Society of Trusts and Estates Practitioners (STEP) Journal
- Private Client Law Review
- Taxation magazine

APPENDIX ONE

STATEMENT OF RECEIPTS AND PAYMENTS

Statement of Receipts and Payments
The Estate of the late Joe Bloggs

A) Assets per Confirmation

Item No	Description	Total Assets per Confirmation £
1	32 Tinsel Drive, Tinseltown, TT1 5SE as more properly described in the Land Register of Scotland Title Number TTT123456 as estimated by Estate Agent	£280,000.00
2	Personal Effects Estimated by the Executors	£500.00
3	The United Bank of Tinseltown PO Box 17235, Edinburgh, EH11 1YH Account No: 12345678	
a	Balance at date of death	£2.02
	Interest accrued to date of death but not yet paid	£0.08
b	Account No: 234567891	£9,331.62
	Interest accrued to date of death but not yet paid	£0.00
c	ISA Account No: 345678912	£162.12
	Interest accrued to date of death but not yet paid	£0.46
	Total Assets at Date of Death (A)	**£289,996.30**

LESS:

B) Debts & Funeral Expenses

Item No	Description	£
1	Tinseltown Social Care Account Reference: 123456P Outstanding social care bill to date of death	(£159.00)
2	Tinseltown Health Care Outstanding care home bill to date of death	(£3,250.00)
3	Tinseltown Funeral Parlour Funeral	(£6,100.75)
	Total Debts & Funeral Expenses at Date of Death (B)	**(£9,509.75)**

LESS:
C) Adjustments to Confirmation

1	32 Tinsel Drive, Tinseltown, TT1 5SE Loss on sale price achieved within 12 months of death	(£50,000.00)
2	Tinseltown Council Refund of overpaid Council Tax	£3,894.71
3	The United Bank of Tinseltown ISA Account No: 345678912 Gain on account due to incorrect date of death value being supplie	£36.10
	Total Adjustments to Confirmation (C)	**(£46,069.19)**
	Net Estate for Inheritance Tax Purposes (D) (A-B-C)	**£234,417.36**

ADD:
E) Sundry Receipts

tem N	Description		£
1	Scottish Public Pensions Agency NHS Pension Payment		£108.45
2	Josephine Bloggs Payments introduced to meet costs of administration of estate		
a	ABC Solicitors		
	02/10/2024	Payment of invoice 35509 (Multi search)	£234.00
	27/08/2024	Payment of invoice 35271 (Cash)	£283.00
	09/05/2024	Payment of invoice 34752 (Various)	£366.00
b	General Expenses for the renovation and clearance of 32 Tinsel Drive		£1,228.47
		Total Sundry Receipts (E)	**£2,219.92**

LESS:
F) Administration Expenses

Item No	Description	£
1	Scottish Courts & Tribunals Service Confirmation dues	(£573.00)
2	ABC Solicitors	
a	Interim fee for the administration of the estate	(£2,250.00)
	VAT due thereon @ 20%	(£450.00)
b	Final fee for administration of estate Restricted to:	(£6,000.00)

	VAT due thereon @ 20%	(£1,200.00)
2	ABC Solicitors (cont'd)	
c	Anti money laundering fee	(£30.00)
	VAT due thereon @ 20%	(£6.00)
3	West Dunbartonshire Council	
	Death certificate for Joseph Bloggs (junior) and postage	(£15.85)
4	Glasgow City Council	
	Death certificate for Edward Bloggs and postage	(£16.10)
5	TM Property Searches	
	Multisearch Report Fee	(£234.00)
6	Registers of Scotland	
a	Fee for Advance Notice	(£20.00)
b	Registration dues of discharge of Standard Security	(£80.00)
c	Books of Council and Session Registration Fee	(£20.00)
7	Tinseltown Estate Agents	
	Estate Agents Fee including home report	(£3,658.80)
8	B & Q	
	Sundry receipts for renovation and clearance of 32 Tinsel Drive	(£28.50)
9	The Range	
a	Sundry receipts for renovation and clearance of 32 Tinsel Drive	(£38.54)
b	Sundry receipts for renovation and clearance of 32 Tinsel Drive	(£69.43)
10	AMA Waste Management	
a	Waste management fee for clearance of property at 32 Tinsel Driv	(£312.00)
b	Waste management fee for clearance of property at 32 Tinsel Driv	(£390.00)
c	Waste management fee for clearance of property at 32 Tinsel Driv	(£390.00)
11	Scottish Public Pensions Agency	
	Overpayment of NHS Pension	(£108.45)
12	Josephine Bloggs	
	Refund of sums due to her in respect of cash introduced to estate to meet costs	(£2,111.47)
	Total Tax and Expenses of Administration (F)	**(£18,002.14)**

Estate available for Division (D+E-F)					**£218,635.14**
Divisible thus:					
1 Josephine Bloggs					
50% of the residue		£ 109,317.57			
Payable thus:					
A) Assets transferred:					
Personal Effects					
Estimated by the Executors			£ 500.00		
The United Bank of Tinseltown					
PO Box 17235, Edinburgh, EH11 1YH					
Account No: 12345678					
Balance at date of death			£ 2.02		
Interest accrued to date of death but not yet paid			£ 0.08		
Account No: 234567891			£ 9,331.62		
Interest accrued to date of death but not yet paid			£ -		
B) Cash					
Interim payment	Nov-24		£ 82,000.00		
Cash due now			£ 17,483.85	£	109,317.57
2 Jessica Bloggs					
25% of the residue		£ 54,658.79			
Payable thus:					
Interim payment	Nov-24		£ 41,000.00		
Cash due now			£ 13,658.79	£	54,658.79
3 Jason Bloggs					
25% of the residue		£ 54,658.79			
Payable thus:					
Interim payment	Nov-24		£ 41,000.00		
Cash due now			£ 13,658.79	£	54,658.79
		Total Residue distributed		**£**	**218,635.14**

Notes:

1. The Deceased, Joe Bloggs, died on 13 February 2024 leaving a Will dated 6 June 2009 and registered in the Books of Council & Session on 21 May 2024 which appointed Josephine Bloggs as his Executor.
2. Confirmation to the estate was recorded by Dumbarton Sheriff Court on 19 August 2024.
3 Under the terms of the Will, a legacy of the deceased's house, free of expenses, was left to Edward Bloggs and Joseph Bloggs (junior) with the residue of the estate being divided among Josephine Bloggs, Jessica Bloggs and Jason Bloggs.
4. Both Edward Bloggs and Joseph Bloggs (junior) predeceased the deceased leaving no issue. Accordingly, the legacy fell in terms of the provisions of the Will and the asset forms part of the residue.

APPENDIX TWO

ACCOUNT OF CHARGE AND DISCHARGE

Account of Charge and Discharge
In the Estate of the Late Imelda Smith

Prepared for the Executor by
MBA Solicitors
175 Anywhere Street
Anytown

Ref: DFG/SAS/BLOGJ12345

ACCOUNT of CHARGE and DISCHARGE
of the intromissions of the Executor

FROM 06 March 2019

TO 18 April 2024

CHARGE		**£**	**£**	**£**
I	**ESTATE AT DATE OF DEATH**			
	19b Acacia Avenue, Anytown			
	Valued by Anytown Surveyors at		£ 35,000.00	
	Cash			
	Found in house	£ 3,569.88		
	Held in solicitors client account	£ 16,902.69	£ 20,472.57	£ 55,472.57
II	**ESTATE ALLOTTED**			
	Nil			
III	**ESTATE REVALUED**			
	Nil			
IV	**ESTATE REALISED**	Book Value	Realised	
	19b Acacia Avenue, Anytown	£ 35,000.00	£ 93,250.00	
		£ 35,000.00	£ 93,250.00	
	Gain on Realisation	£ 58,250.00		£ 58,250.00
		£ 93,250.00	£ 93,250.00	
V	**INTEREST**			
	MBA Solicitors			
	Client account			
	Interest to 01/04/2019	£ 7.90		
	Interest to 01/05/2019	£ 7.64		
	Interest to 01/06/2019	£ 8.36		
	Interest to 01/07/2019	£ 7.37		
	C/F	£ 31.27		£ 113,722.57

				£	£	£
V	**INTEREST (Cont'd)**					
			B/F	£ 31.27		£ 113,722.57
	MBA Solicitors (Cont'd)					
	Client account					
	Interest to	01/08/2019		£ 8.22		
	Interest to	01/09/2019		£ 8.42		
	Interest to	01/10/2019		£ 7.97		
	Interest to	01/11/2019		£ 8.68		
	Interest to	01/12/2019		£ 8.68		
	Interest to	01/01/2020		£ 9.04		
	Interest to	01/02/2020		£ 9.51		
	Interest to	01/03/2020		£ 8.32		
	Interest to	01/04/2020		£ 4.25		
	Interest to	01/02/2022		£ 5.38		
	Interest to	01/03/2022		£ 3.20		
	Interest to	01/04/2022		£ 2.10		
	Interest to	01/05/2022		£ 7.56		
	Interest to	31/05/2022		£ 7.82		
	Interest to	01/07/2022		£ 15.82		
	Interest to	01/08/2022		£ 14.94		
	Interest to	01/09/2022		£ 21.40		
	Interest to	01/10/2022		£ 23.47		
	Interest to	01/11/2022		£ 29.28		
	Interest to	01/12/2022		£ 38.08		
	Interest to	01/01/2023		£ 44.10		
	Interest to	01/02/2023		£ 47.46		
	Interest to	01/03/2023		£ 49.02		
	Interest to	01/04/2023		£ 55.42		
	Interest to	01/05/2023		£ 56.27		
	Interest to	01/06/2023		£ 58.60		
	Interest to	01/07/2023		£ 59.16		
	Interest to	01/08/2023		£ 66.18		
	Interest to	01/09/2023		£ 69.70		
	Interest to	01/10/2023		£ 63.11		
	Interest to	01/11/2023		£ 64.90		
	Interest to	01/12/2023		£ 61.74		
	Interest to	01/01/2024		£ 62.42		
	Interest to	01/02/2024		£ 34.36		
	Interest to close			£ 734.00	£ 1,799.85	£ 1,799.85
VI	**RENT**					
	Rent to	31/05/2019		£ 1,112.50		
	Backdated rent			£ 12,237.50	£ 13,350.00	£ 13,350.00
			C/F		£ 13,350.00	£ 128,872.42

	B/F		£ 13,350.00	£ 128,872.42
VII	**MISCELLANEOUS**	**£**	**£**	**£**
	Anytown Council			
	Refund of overpaid Council Tax on sale		£ 230.59	£ 230.59
	SUM OF THE CHARGE			**£ 129,103.01**

DISCHARGE		**£**	**£**	**£**
I	**EXPENSES OF ADMINISTRATION**			
	MBA Solicitors			
30/08/2020	Interim fee for the administration of the estate (including VAT)	£ 3,600.00		
14/02/2022	Interim fee for the administration of the estate (including VAT)	£ 2,340.00		
18/04/2024	Final fee for the administration of the estate (including VAT)	£ 8,137.63	£ 14,077.63	
	Anytown Insurance Services			
09/10/2023	Home Insurance		£ 390.61	
	Anytown Boiler Services			
02/02/2024	Service and parts		£ 192.00	
	Anytown Factors Limited			
05/05/2023	Factoring fee	£ 72.99		
05/08/2023	Factoring fee	£ 256.33		
05/11/2023	Factoring fee	£ 276.43		
05/11/2023	Common Charges Fee	£ 690.01		
13/12/2023	Replacement key for back communal door	£ 36.14		
05/02/2024	Common Charges Fee	£ 863.32	£ 2,195.22	
	Anytown Council			
17/02/2020	Landlord Registration Fee	£ 59.40		
03/04/2021	Council Tax	£ 152.56		
14/04/2022	Council Tax 2022/2023	£ 1,156.74		
03/04/2023	Council Tax 2023/2024 (inc unoccupancy premium)	£ 2,710.29	£ 4,078.99	
	Anytown Energy			
18/03/2024	Closing balance		£ 413.49	
	Registers of Scotland			
30/04/2019	Registers Direct Search	£ 7.20		
15/02/2023	Copy Title Sheet	£ 20.00	£ 27.20	
26/03/2024	Anytown Locksmith			
	Locksmith invoice		£ 216.00	£ 21,591.14
	C/F			£ 21,591.14

	B/F			£ 21,591.14
II	**EXPENSES ON SALE OF 19b ACACIA AVENUE, ANYTOWN**	**£**	**£**	**£**
	MBA Solicitors			
01/04/2024	Fee for the sale of the property (including VAT)		£ 2,340.00	
	Anytown Estate Agents			
11/11/2023	Marketing Fee	£ 360.00		
01/04/2024	Estate Agency Fee	£ 1,500.00	£ 1,860.00	
	Anytown Surveyors			
15/11/2023	Home Report		£ 360.00	
	Registers of Scotland			
01/03/2024	Advance Notice	£ 20.00		
01/03/2024	Scotlis Searches	£ 10.80		
01/03/2024	Scotlis Title Report	£ 30.00	£ 60.80	
	First Scottish			
01/03/2024	Multisearch & Coal Report		£ 222.00	£ 4,842.80
III	**PAYMENTS TO BENEFICIARIES**			
	Claire Carroll			
	25% share of the residue		£ 25,667.27	
	Christina MacLean			
	5% share of the residue		£ 5,133.45	
	Derek Carmichael			
	30% share of the residue		£ 30,800.72	
	Jacob Sharp			
	10% share of the residue		£ 10,266.91	
	Lucy Sharp			
	10% share of the residue		£ 10,266.91	
	Angela McGhee			
	20% of the residue		£ 20,533.81	£ 102,669.07
	SUM OF THE DISCHARGE			**£ 129,103.01**

APPENDIX THREE

FULL ESTATE ACCOUNTS

Joe Bloggs
as
Executor of the late Josephine Bloggs

Account of the Intromissions of the Estate
from
11 June 2023 (date of death)
to
20 September 2024 (close of estate)

Prepared for the Executor by
ABC Solicitors
189 Anywhere Street
Anytown

Ref: AM/BLOGGS12345

Synopsis

Testator:	Josephine Bloggs	
Date of Death:	11-Jun-23	
Date of Will:	04-May-18	
Date of Codicil:	26-Apr-23	
Date of Confirmation:	08-Mar-24 Dumbaton Sheriff Court	
Specific Legacies:	John Pearson	5 Acacia Avenue, Anytown
Pecuniary Legacies:	Devon MacDonald	£10,000
	Chloe MacDonald	£10,000
Residue:	100% to Pansy Hunter	

For full details of the provisions of the Estate, please see the Will and Codicil.

Notes:
1. There was a legacy of shares in Neither Here Nor There Limited to Imelda Smith contained in the Will.
At the time of her death, the deceased did not own any shares in the Company and therefore the legacy lapsed.
2. The deceased died unmarried and without children or remoter issue and therefore legal rights claims did not apply in this estate.

Summary

Estate per Confirmation	Schedule One - Branch I	£548,838.22
ADD:		
Adjustments to Confirmation	Schedule One - Branch II	£286,904.90
LESS:		
Funeral Expenses & Debts	Schedule Two	(£89,292.59)
	Net Estate for Inheritance Tax purposes	**£746,450.53**
ADD:		
Sundry Receipts	Schedule Three	£15,153.23
Gain on Realisation	Schedule One - Branch VI	£22,430.00
LESS:		
Accrued income written off & reflected in income Schedule (Schedule Four)	Schedule One - Branch V	(£57.12)
Expenses	Schedule Five	(£111,621.88)
Legacies	Schedule Six	(£215,000.00)
	Net Capital Estate	**£457,354.76**
ADD:		
Income	Schedule Four	£3,705.08
	Total Estate available for Distribution as Residue Transferred to Schedule Seven	**£461,059.84**

Schedule One - Capital

Item No	Description	Branch I Assets per Confirmation	Branch II Adjustments to Confirmation	Branch III Assets Transferred	Branch IV Assets Realised	Branch V Accrued income written off and reflected in Income Schedule	Branch VI Gain/Loss on Realisation
1	19a Acacia Avenue, Anytown						
	As valued by Anytown Residential	£245,000.00			£267,500.00		£22,500.00
2	5 Acacia Avenue, Anytown						
	As valued by Anytown Residential	£195,000.00		£195,000.00			£0.00
3	South Anytown Council						
	Refund of Council Tax	£738.76	(£738.76)				£0.00
4	Royal Bank of Anytown						
a	Account No: 001234/87654321						
	Balance at date of death	£2,790.38			£2,790.38		£0.00
	Interest accrued to date of death but not yet paid	£0.00			£0.00	£0.00	£0.00
b	Account No: 001234/98765432						
	Balance at date of death	£5,031.13			£5,031.13		£0.00
	Interest accrued to date of death but not yet paid	£1.38			£0.00	(£1.38)	£0.00
Balance carried forward		**£448,561.65**	(£738.76)	**£195,000.00**	**£275,321.51**	(£1.38)	**£22,500.00**

Item No	Description	Branch I	Branch II	Branch III	Branch IV	Branch V	Branch VI
Balance brought forward		**£448,561.65**	(£738.76)	**£195,000.00**	**£275,321.51**	(£1.38)	**£22,500.00**
		Assets per Confirmation	Adjustments to Confirmation	Assets Transferred	Assets Realised	Accrued income written off and reflected in Income Schedule	Gain/Loss on Realisation
4 (Cont'd)	Royal Bank of Anytown						
c	Account No: 001234/0876543						
	Balance at date of death	£100,220.83			£100,220.83		£0.00
	Interest accrued to date of death but not yet paid	£55.74			£0.00	(£55.74)	£0.00
5	Bananaman Inc PLC 4,999 Ordinary shares		£282,224.00	£282,224.00			£0.00
6	Anytown Pension Scheme Pension ID: MEM000000001 Death benefits due to estate		£2,071.00		£2,071.00		£0.00
7	Personal effects as value by Anytown Auctioneers		£770.00	£700.00			(£70.00)
8	Neither Here Not There Limited Final salary/accrued holidays payment		£2,485.91		£2,485.91		£0.00
9	TV Licence Refund		£92.75		£92.75		£0.00
Balance carried forward		**£548,838.22**	**£286,904.90**	**£477,924.00**	**£380,192.00**	(£57.12)	**£22,430.00**

Item No	Description	Branch I Assets per Confirmation	Branch II Adjustments to Confirmation	Branch III Assets Transferred	Branch IV Assets Realised	Branch V Accrued income written off and reflected in Income Schedule	Branch VI Gain/Loss on Realisation
Balance brought forward		£548,838.22	£286,904.90	£477,924.00	£380,192.00	(£57.12)	£22,430.00
Balance brought forward		£548,838.22	£286,904.90	£477,924.00	£380,192.00	(£57.12)	£22,430.00
Branch I	Total Assets per Confirmation	£548,838.22					
Branch II	Total Adjustments to Confirmation		£286,904.90				
Branch III	Total Assets Transferred			£477,924.00			
Branch IV	Total Assets Realised				£380,192.00		
Branch V	Total Accrued Income written off					(£57.12)	
Branch VI	Total Gain/Loss on Realisation						£22,430.00

Schedule Two - Funeral Expenses & Debts

Item No	Description	£
1	Anytown Independent Funeral Services	
	Funeral	£ 4,577.00
2	The Anytown Hotel	
	Funeral Tea	£ 3,099.85
3	Royal Bank of Anytown	
a	Mortgage	£ 74,683.20
b	Personal Loan	£ 4,869.11
4	HM Revenues and Customs	
a	Income Tax due for year 2022/2023	£ 1,201.23
b	Income Tax due to date of death	£ 789.48
5	Anytown Factors Limited	
	Factoring invoice due to date of death	£ 72.72
	Total	**£ 89,292.59**

Schedule Three - Sundry Receipts

Item No	Description		£
1	Joe Bloggs		
	Funds introduced to pay for the following		
a	Vetinary Medicine for Lowell (the dog)		
i	26/06/2023 Invoice	£	31.30
ii	06/07/2023 Invoice	£	66.96
ii	20/07/2023 Invoice	£	111.59
iv	24/08/2023 Invoice	£	100.12
v	31/08/2023 Invoice	£	104.94
vi	01/09/2023 Invoice	£	43.32
vii	18/09/2023 Invoice	£	82.32
viii	16/10/2023 Invoice	£	143.87
ix	02/11/2023 Invoice	£	143.44
x	05/11/2023 Cremation Invoice	£	425.00
b	Property Expenses		
i	Anytown Tiler	£	860.00
ii	Tile Superstore - Tiles	£	122.00
ii	B & Q - Backdoor	£	30.00
iv	B & Q - Wood facings and glue	£	34.00
v	B & Q - Glass for back door	£	320.00
vi	B & M - Paint	£	17.47
vii	Morrisons - Roller kit	£	16.99
viii	B & Q - floor board	£	20.06
ix	B & Q - Beading	£	21.99
x	B & M - Paint and brush	£	25.69
xi	B & Q - Beading	£	17.59
xii	Gardener from 11/05/2023 to 1/11/2023 @ £30 per visits	£	390.00
xiii	Window Cleaner from 11/05/2023 to 1/11/2023 @ £15 per visits	£	135.00
xvi	B & Q - Light switch	£	34.00
xvii	B & Q - pipes	£	20.00
c	Anytown clearance - skip hire	£	1,000.00
2	Annette Pearson		
	Funds introduced to pay for the following		
a	Funeral	£	4,577.00
b	Funeral Tea	£	3,099.85
3	John Pearson		
	Funds introduced to pay for the following		
a	Home Insurance	£	740.72
4	Anytown Insurance Agency		
	Refund of overpaid premiums	£	19.04
Balance carried forward		**£**	**12,754.26**

Item No	Description	£
Balance brought forward		**£ 12,754.26**
5	Royal Bank of Anytown	
a	Refund of overdraft interest charged	£ 62.20
b	Refund of personal loan non payment fees	£ 747.68
6	Anytown Pet Insurance	
	Refund of premiums paid on cancellation	£ 1,460.59
7	Anytown Factors Limited	
	Refund of factors fees on sale	£ 128.50
	Total	**£ 15,153.23**

Q q

Schedule Four - Income Schedule

Year 1 - Tax Year 2023/2024			
Description	Gross income	Tax Deducted at Source	Net Income
A) Tax Free Income			
Nil	£ -	£ -	£ -
Total Tax Free Income	**£ -**	**£ -**	**£ -**
B) Executry Dividend Tax Rate (8.75%)			
Nil	£ -	£ -	£ -
Total Dividend Tax Rate Income	**£ -**	**£ -**	**£ -**
Tax due on Gross Dividend Income	£ -		
Tax paid at source	£ -		
Tax due now	**£ -**		
C) Executry Tax Rate (other income) (20%)			
Royal Bank of Anytown			
Account No: 001234/98765432			
Interest	£ 72.11	£ -	£ 72.11
Account No: 001234/0876543			
Interest	£ 2,039.54	£ -	£ 2,039.54
Other income Tax Rate Income	**£ 2,111.65**	**£ -**	**£ 2,111.65**
Tax due on Executry Other income	£ 422.33		
Tax paid at source	£ -		
Tax due now	**£ 422.33**		
Total Net Income Received for Tax Year	**£ 2,111.65**		

Year 2 - Tax Year 2024/2025

Description	Gross income	Tax Deducted at Source	Net Income
A) Tax Free Income			
Nil	£ -	£ -	£ -
Total Tax Free Income	**£ -**	**£ -**	**£ -**
B) Executry Dividend Tax Rate (8.75%)			
Nil	£ -	£ -	£ -
Total Dividend Tax Rate Income	**£ -**	**£ -**	**£ -**
Tax due on Gross Dividend Income	£ -		
Tax paid at source	£ -		
Tax due now	**£ -**		
C) Executry Tax Rate (other income) (20%)			
Royal Bank of Anytown			
Account No: 001234/98765432			
Interest	£ 7.55	£ -	£ 7.55
Account No: 001234/0876543			
Interest	£ 1,585.88	£ -	£ 1,585.88
Other income Tax Rate Income	**£ 1,593.43**	**£ -**	**£ 1,593.43**
Tax due on Executry Other income	£ 318.69		
Tax paid at source	£ -		
Tax due now	**£ 318.69**		
Total Net Income Received for Tax Year	**£ 1,593.43**		
Total overall net income received	**£ 3,705.08**		

Schedule Five - Tax and Expenses of Administration Schedule

Item No	Description		£
1	Anytown Auctioneers		
	Contents valuation	£	240.00
2	Vetinary Medicine for Lowell (the dog)		
a	26/06/2023 Invoice	£	31.30
b	06/07/2023 Invoice	£	66.96
c	20/07/2023 Invoice	£	111.59
d	24/08/2023 Invoice	£	100.12
e	31/08/2023 Invoice	£	104.94
f	01/09/2023 Invoice	£	43.32
g	18/09/2023 Invoice	£	82.32
h	16/10/2023 Invoice	£	143.87
i	02/11/2023 Invoice	£	143.44
j	05/11/2023 Cremation invoice	£	425.00
3	Property Expenses		
a	Anytown Tiler	£	860.00
b	Tile Superstore - Tiles	£	122.00
c	B & Q - Backdoor	£	30.00
d	B & Q - Wood facings and glue	£	34.00
e	B & Q - Glass for back door	£	320.00
f	B & M - Paint	£	17.47
g	Morrisons - Roller kit	£	16.99
h	B & Q - floor board	£	20.06
i	B & Q - Beading	£	21.99
j	B & M - Paint and brush	£	25.69
k	B & Q - Beading	£	17.59
l	Gardener from 11/05/2023 to 1/11/2023 @ £30 per visits	£	390.00
m	Window Cleaner from 11/05/2023 to 1/11/2023 @ £15 per visits	£	135.00
n	B & Q - Light switch	£	34.00
o	B & Q - pipes	£	20.00
p	Anytown clearance - skip hire	£	1,000.00
4	Joe Bloggs		
a	Refund of outlays	£	3,317.65
b	Refund of outlays	£	1,000.00
5	Annette Pearson		
	Refund of outlays	£	7,676.85
6	John Pearson		
	Refund of outlays	£	740.72
Balance carried forward		**£**	**17,292.87**

Item No	Description	£
Balance brought forward		**£ 17,292.87**
7	Anytown Insurance Agency	
	Home insurance	£ 740.72
8	Anytown Energy PLC	
	Final energy bill	£ 2,097.56
9	Registers of Scotland	
a	Title search	£ 3.60
b	Advance notice	£ 20.00
c	Discharge of security dues	£ 60.00
d	Disposition registration dues	£ 400.00
e	Title search/sheets x 2	£ 7.20
f	Deed Registration	£ 20.00
10	Anytown Factors Limited	
	Final factors bill	£ 422.18
11	ABC solicitors	
a	Interim fee for the administration of the estate	£ 6,330.00
	VAT thereon @ 20%	£ 1,266.00
b	Interim fee for the administration of the estate	£ 3,965.00
	VAT thereon @ 20%	£ 793.00
c	Interim fee for the administration of the estate	£ 610.00
	VAT thereon @ 20%	£ 122.00
d	Final fee for the administration of the estate	£ 3,947.50
	VAT thereon @ 20%	£ 789.50
12	Anytown Estate Agents	
	Estate Agent fee for the sale of the property	£ 2,988.00
13	Scottish Courts and Tribunals Service	
	Confirmation fees	£ 578.00
14	HMRC	
a	Inheritance Tax	£ 60,090.62
b	Income Tax due for the period of administration	£ 741.02
c	Capital Gains Tax due for the period of administration - 2024/2025	£ 2,137.83
15	Royal Bank of Anytown	
	Personal Loan - final payment adjustment	£ 30.24
Balance carried forward		**£ 105,452.83**

Item No	Description	£
Balance brought forward		**£ 105,452.83**
17	Royal Bank of Anytown	
	Account No: 001234/0876543	
	Debits from account post death prior to freezing	
a	Whatever Happens/Who knows?	£ 48.00
b	Disney +	£ 7.99
c	Currys	£ 10.80
d	Apple	£ 272.00
e	Ring	£ 13.96
f	Apple	£ 47.52
g	Eon	£ 601.59
h	Hastings Insurance	£ 26.34
i	South Anytime Council	£ 749.98
j	Royal Bank of Anytown Mortgages	£ 1,667.51
k	Pet Plan Limited	£ 110.89
l	Churchill Pet	£ 308.36
m	Direct Line	£ 20.10
n	Royal Bank of Anytown personal loan	£ 747.68
o	BG Services	£ 53.00
p	Sky	£ 129.50
q	TV Licence	£ 13.25
r	Animal Friends	£ 50.52
s	Overdraft interest	£ 72.37
18	Anytown Council	
	Completion certificate	£ 27.05
19	Eagle Couriers	
a	Courier charges	£ 237.90
b	Courier charges	£ 379.80
c	Courier charges	£ 36.60
20	First Scottish	
a	Multisearch	£ 182.00
b	Legal report	£ 49.00
21	ABC Plumbers	
	Plumbers invoice	£ 140.00
22	Royal Mail	
a	Courier charges	£ 67.67
b	Courier charges	£ 67.67
Balance carried forward		**£ 111,591.88**

Item No	Description	£
Balance brought forward		**£ 111,591.88**
23	CBA Solicitors Bank charge on remitting fuds for sale	£ 30.00
	Total Tax and Expenses of Administration	**£ 111,621.88**

Schedule Six - Legacies

Item No	Beneficiary	Description	£
1	Devon MacDonald	Cash	£ 10,000.00
2	Chloe MacDonald	Cash	£ 10,000.00
3	John Pearson	5 Acacia Avenue, Anytown	£ 195,000.00
		Total Tax and Expenses of Administration	**£ 215,000.00**

Schedule Seven - Residue Beneficiary Statement

Capital Brought Forward from Summary			£ 457,354.76
Income Brought Forward from Summary			£ 3,705.08
Total Residue to be Distributed			**£ 461,059.84**
Distributed thus:			
100% to Pansy Hunter	£ 461,059.84		
Assets transferred			
Personal effects		£ 700.00	
Bananaman Inc PLC			
4,999 Ordinary shares		£ 282,224.00	
Cash			
Cash due now		£ 178,135.84	£ 461,059.84
Total Estate Distributed			**£ 461,059.84**

Appendix One - Capital Gains Tax

19a Acacia Avenue, Anytown		
Sale price		£267,500.00
LESS		
Confirmation value		(£245,000.00)
	Gross Gain on sale	**£22,500.00**
LESS:		
Allowable expenses as follows		
A) Executors annual allowance Year 1 - 2023/2024		(£6,000.00)
B) Improvement expenses		
Backdoor	£30.00	
Glass for back door	£320.00	
Wood for floor	£20.06	(£370.06)
C) Costs of Sale		
Registers of Scotland		
Title search	£3.60	
Advance notice	£20.00	
Discharge of security dues	£60.00	
Disposition registration dues	£400.00	
Title search/sheets x 2	£7.20	
ABC Solicitors		
Fee for the sale of the property	£3,965.00	
VAT thereon @ 20%	£793.00	
Anytown Estate Agents		
Estate Agent fee for the sale of the property	£2,988.00	
South Anytown Council		
Completion certificate	£27.05	
First Scottish		
Multisearch	£182.00	
Legal report	£49.00	(£8,494.85)
	Net Gain subject to Tax	£7,635.09
	Tax due thereon at 28%	**£2,137.83**

MORE BOOKS BY
LAW BRIEF PUBLISHING

A selection of our other titles available now:-

'A Practical Guide to Administering Estates and Obtaining Probate in England & Wales' by Stephanie Christie-Carmichael
'A Practical Guide to Probation Breaches and Other Applications' by Mark Thomas
'A Practical Guide to Remarriage and Divorce' by Cordelia Williams & Claire Howard
'A Practical Guide to Privacy, Transparency, Reporting Restrictions and Closed Proceedings in the Court of Protection' by Laura Mannering
'Beaumont on Barristers – A Guide to Defending Disciplinary Proceedings (Second Edition)' by Marc Beaumont
'A Practical Guide to Payments for Environmental Services' by Ben Sharples
'A Practical Guide to the Law of Pregnancy and Maternity at Work' by Rebecca Thomas
'A Practical Guide to Redundancy – Second Edition' by Philip Hyland & Collette Moore
'A Practical Guide to International Issues for Scottish Family Lawyers' by Susie Mountain, Donna McKay, Ken MacDonald
'A Practical Guide to the Law on Deprivation of Liberty' by Ben Troke
'A Practical Guide to Rights over Airspace and Subsoil – Second Edition' by Daniel Gatty
'A Practical Guide to the Law in Relation to Inquests' by Ramya Nagesh
'A Practical Guide to the Construction and Rectification of Wills and Trust Instruments (Second Edition)' by Edward Hewitt
'A Practical Guide to Data Protection in Social Housing' by Clare Paterson
'A Practical Guide to Spousal Maintenance – Second Edition' by Liz Cowell
'A Practical Guide to International Parental Child Abduction Law (England and Wales)' by Dr Onyója Momoh
'A Practical Guide to Deprivation of British Citizenship' by Sean Ell
'A Practical Guide to Commercial Property Service Charges' by Rachel Garton
'A Practical Guide to Clinical Negligence – Third Edition' by Geoffrey Simpson-Scott (Geoff)

'A Practical Guide to the Rights of Grandparents in Children Proceedings – Second Edition' by Stuart Barlow
'The Electronic Communications Code: A Practical Guide – Second Edition' by Kerry Bretherton KC, James Castle, Mark Loveday
'A Practical Guide to the Independent School Standards – September 2023 Edition' by Sarah McKimm
'A Practical Guide to Estate Administration and Crypto Assets' by Richard Marshall
'A Practical Guide to Parental Alienation in Private and Public Law Children Cases' by Sam King QC & Frankie Shama
'Contested Heritage – Removing Art from Land and Historic Buildings' by Richard Harwood QC, Catherine Dobson, David Sawtell
'The Limits of Separate Legal Personality: When Those Running a Company Can Be Held Personally Liable for Losses Caused to Third Parties Outside of the Company' by Dr Mike Wilkinson
'A Practical Guide to Transgender Law' by Robin Moira White & Nicola Newbegin
'A Practical Guide to 'Stranded Spouses' in Family Law' by Mani Singh Basi
'A Practical Guide to Residential Freehold Conveyancing' by Lorraine Richardson
'A Practical Guide to Pensions on Divorce for Lawyers' by Bryan Scant
'A Practical Guide to Challenging Sham Marriage Allegations in Immigration Law' by Priya Solanki
'A Practical Guide to Digital Communications Evidence in Criminal Law' by Sam Willis
'A Practical Guide to Legal Rights in Scotland' by Sarah-Jane Macdonald
'A Practical Guide to New Build Conveyancing' by Paul Sams & Rebecca East
'A Practical Guide to Inherited Wealth on Divorce' by Hayley Trim
'A Practical Guide to Practice Direction 12J and Domestic Abuse in Private Law Children Proceedings' by Rebecca Cross & Malvika Jaganmohan
'A Practical Guide to Confiscation and Restraint' by Narita Bahra QC, John Carl Townsend, David Winch
'A Practical Guide to the Law of Forests in Scotland' by Philip Buchan
'A Practical Guide to Health and Medical Cases in Immigration Law' by Rebecca Chapman & Miranda Butler
'A Practical Guide to Bad Character Evidence for Criminal Practitioners by Aparna Rao
'A Practical Guide to Extradition Law post-Brexit' by Myles Grandison et al

'A Practical Guide to Hoarding and Mental Health for Housing Lawyers' by Rachel Coyle
'Stephens on Contractual Indemnities' by Richard Stephens
'A Practical Guide to the EU Succession Regulation' by Richard Frimston
'A Practical Guide to Solicitor and Client Costs – Second Edition' by Robin Dunne
'Constructive Dismissal – Practice Pointers and Principles' by Benjimin Burgher
'A Practical Guide to Religion and Belief Discrimination Claims in the Workplace' by Kashif Ali
'A Practical Guide to the Law of Medical Treatment Decisions' by Ben Troke
'Fundamental Dishonesty and QOCS in Personal Injury Proceedings: Law and Practice' by Jake Rowley
'A Practical Guide to the Law in Relation to School Exclusions' by Charlotte Hadfield & Alice de Coverley
'A Practical Guide to Divorce for the Silver Separators' by Karin Walker
'The Right to be Forgotten – The Law and Practical Issues' by Melissa Stock
'A Practical Guide to Planning Law and Rights of Way in National Parks, the Broads and AONBs' by James Maurici QC, James Neill et al
'A Practical Guide to Election Law' by Tom Tabori
'A Practical Guide to the Law in Relation to Surrogacy' by Andrew Powell
'A Practical Guide to Claims Arising from Fatal Accidents – Second Edition' by James Patience
'A Practical Guide to Asbestos Claims' by Jonathan Owen & Gareth McAloon
'A Practical Guide to Stamp Duty Land Tax in England and Northern Ireland' by Suzanne O'Hara
'A Practical Guide to the Law of Farming Partnerships' by Philip Whitcomb
'A Practical Guide to the Law of Unlawful Eviction and Harassment – Second Edition' by Stephanie Lovegrove
'A Practical Guide to Costs in Personal Injury Claims – Second Edition' by Matthew Hoe
'A Practical Guide to the General Data Protection Regulation (GDPR) – Second Edition' by Keith Markham
'A Practical Guide to Working with Litigants in Person and McKenzie Friends in Family Cases' by Stuart Barlow
'Protecting Unregistered Brands: A Practical Guide to the Law of Passing Off' by Lorna Brazell

'A Practical Guide to Secondary Liability and Joint Enterprise Post-Jogee' by Joanne Cecil & James Mehigan

'A Practical Guide to the Pre-Action RTA Claims Protocol for Personal Injury Lawyers' by Antonia Ford

'A Practical Guide to Neighbour Disputes and the Law' by Alexander Walsh

'A Practical Guide to Coercive Control for Legal Practitioners and Victims' by Rachel Horman

'A Practical Guide to the Law of Driverless Cars – Second Edition'

by Alex Glassbrook, Emma Northey & Scarlett Milligan

'A Practical Guide to TOLATA Claims' by Greg Williams

'A Practical Guide to Elderly Law – Second Edition' by Justin Patten

'A Practical Guide to Responding to Housing Disrepair and Unfitness Claims' by Iain Wightwick

'A Practical Guide to the Law of Bullying and Harassment in the Workplace' by Philip Hyland

'How to Be a Freelance Solicitor: A Practical Guide to the SRA-Regulated Freelance Solicitor Model' by Paul Bennett

'A Practical Guide to Prison Injury Claims' by Malcolm Johnson

'A Practical Guide to Advising Clients at the Police Station' by Colin Stephen McKeown-Beaumont

'A Practical Guide to Antisocial Behaviour Injunctions – Second Edition' by Iain Wightwick

'Practical Mediation: A Guide for Mediators, Advocates, Advisers, Lawyers, and Students in Civil, Commercial, Business, Property, Workplace, and Employment Cases' by Jonathan Dingle with John Sephton

'The Mini-Pupillage Workbook' by David Boyle

'A Practical Guide to Crofting Law' by Brian Inkster

'A Practical Guide to the Law of Domain Names and Cybersquatting' by Andrew Clemson

'A Practical Guide to the Law of Gender Pay Gap Reporting' by Harini Iyengar

'NHS Whistleblowing and the Law' by Joseph England

'Employment Law and the Gig Economy' by Nigel Mackay & Annie Powell

'A Practical Guide to Noise Induced Hearing Loss (NIHL) Claims' by Andrew Mckie, Ian Skeate, Gareth McAloon

'An Introduction to Beauty Negligence Claims – A Practical Guide for the Personal Injury Practitioner' by Greg Almond

'Intercompany Agreements for Transfer Pricing Compliance' by Paul Sutton

'Zen and the Art of Mediation' by Martin Plowman
'A Practical Guide to Adoption for Family Lawyers' by Graham Pegg
'A Practical Guide to Industrial Disease Claims' by Andrew Mckie & Ian Skeate
'A Practical Guide to Conducting a Sheriff Court Proof' by Andrew Stevenson
'A Practical Guide to Vicarious Liability' by Mariel Irvine
'A Practical Guide to Applications for Landlord's Consent and Variation of Leases' by Mark Shelton
'A Practical Guide to Relief from Sanctions Post-Mitchell and Denton' by Peter Causton
'A Practical Guide to Equity Release for Advisors' by Paul Sams
'A Practical Guide to Financial Services Claims' by Chris Hegarty
'A Practical Guide to Financial Ombudsman Service Claims' by Adam Temple & Robert Scrivenor
'A Practical Guide to Running Housing Disrepair and Cavity Wall Claims – Second Edition' by Andrew Mckie & Ian Skeate
'A Practical Guide to Holiday Sickness Claims – Second Edition' by Andrew Mckie & Ian Skeate
'Arguments and Tactics for Personal Injury and Clinical Negligence Claims' by Dorian Williams
'A Practical Guide to Drone Law' by Rufus Ballaster, Andrew Firman, Eleanor Clot
'On Experts: CPR35 for Lawyers and Experts' by David Boyle
'An Introduction to Personal Injury Law' by David Boyle

www.ingramcontent.com/pod-product-compliance
Lightning Source LLC
LaVergne TN
LVHW052303200926
848481LV00002B/450
* 9 7 8 1 9 1 6 6 9 8 7 9 6 *